THE BEGINNER'S GUIDE
TO MAKING WINE
FROM JUICE AND GRAPES

Modern Home Winemaking
A Guide to Making Consistently Great Wines

❖

Techniques in Home Winemaking
The Comprehensive Guide to Making Château-Style Wines

❖

Kit Winemaking
The Illustrated Beginner's Guide to Making Wine from Concentrate

❖

Wine Myths, Facts & Snobberies
81 Questions & Answers on the Science and Enjoyment of Wine

THE BEGINNER'S GUIDE

TO MAKING WINE

FROM JUICE AND GRAPES

DANIEL PAMBIANCHI

Véhicule Press

Published with the generous assistance of the Canada Book Fund of the Department of Canadian Heritage.

Canadä

Cover design: David Drummond
Typeset by David Leblanc of studio oneonone
Technical editing by Robert Peak
Illustrations by Don Martin

Library and Archives Canada Cataloguing in Publication

Title: The beginner's guide to making wine from juice and grapes / Daniel
    Pambianchi.
Names: Pambianchi, Daniel, author.
Description: Includes index.
Identifiers: Canadiana 20230585779 | ISBN 9781550656398 (softcover)
Subjects: LCSH: Wine and wine making—Amateurs' manuals. | LCGFT:
    Handbooks and manuals.
Classification: LCC TP548.2 .P36 2024 | DDC 641.87/2—dc23

Published by Véhicule Press, Montréal, Québec, Canada

Distribution in Canada by LitDistCo
www.litdistco.ca

Distribution in the U.S.by Independent Publishers Group
ipgbook.com

Printed in Canada on FSC®-certified paper.

Disclaimer

Additives, processing aids, reagents and other products and chemicals referenced in this book have applications in winemaking, wine analysis, and sanitization. With care and caution, these can be safely used in home winemaking although some may be unsafe or may pose a health hazard if not used in the recommended concentrations or if used by unskilled winemakers.

Neither the author, editors, or the publisher assumes any responsibility for the use or misuse of information contained in this book.

References to winemaking supplies from various manufacturers or vendors are included to illustrate typical use of these supplies from companies whose products are the most prevalent in the home winemaking market. The use of these references and all trademarks and copyrighted material from cited manufacturers, suppliers, wholesalers, retailers, distributors or other constitute neither sponsorship nor affiliation of these companies with the author, editors and publisher, or with this book. Companies have not paid any promotional fees to have their names and/or products listed here.

Contents

Foreword

I first started making wine in 1963 when I found Grandma's recipe for dandelion wine. I went to the hardware store, bought my first hydrometer, and set out excitedly to make my first batch of wine! It turned out cloudy and harsh, but as soon as fermentation was done my friends and I drank every drop and loved it. As I look back it was a proud moment!

Home winemaking knowledge was very limited six decades ago. No internet, no home computers, no social media to reach out to other amateur winemakers. I wasn't even able to find a book on the subject in the library, though a few did exist.

Hobby winemakers today have access to a wealth of information, all at our fingertips. But it was through several mentors, including Daniel Pambianchi, that my knowledge and enthusiasm has grown, along with the quality of my wines, which have become some of my best ever! Daniel's mentorship in our social media groups and his extensive writings have helped home winemakers make far better wines. He explains the science behind the craft. We can better understand and appreciate the reasons for using wine additives and processing equipment, and making better, more informed decisions.

When I read reviews on Daniel's first book, *Techniques in Home Winemaking*, I bought a copy and read every word! It is very well-written and understandable, but I had to read it more than once. There's so much great and valuable information in it and it is one of my go-to reference books for winemaking!

Daniel has since published *Modern Home Winemaking*, a comprehensive guide for seasoned and advanced winemakers. Those who desire to delve into the technical aspects and learn modern techniques will be thrilled to have this guide.

The Beginner's Guide to Making Wine from Juice and Grapes—Daniel's new book—makes it easy for beginners to venture into making their first and following batches of wine. Daniel introduces all aspects of home winemaking, including the use of additives and processing equipment, basic wine analysis to monitor and ensure quality, along with detailed instructions for making white, rosé and red wines from juice and grapes. I sure wish I had this book 60 years ago! I know you will enjoy Daniel's new book!

Wade Clark
March 2024

Wade Clark is a respected authority on all aspects of home winemaking. He has been a significant contributor to the very successful internet-based group, WinePress.US, as well as helping the popular Home Made Wine Making Facebook group grow to over 54,000 members. He lives in Port Barre, Louisiana.

Icons Used in This Book

Throughout this guide, you will find notes, warnings, tips, and other important information highlighted with the following icons to draw specific attention to important points.

 A short explanation or additional information that you may find useful.

 A warning which, if not observed, can result in unexpected or undesirable outcomes or become a health hazard.

 A useful practical tip that can improve efficiency or simplify a certain procedure.

 Specific advice or instructions for performing a procedure to avoid potential problems.

Glossary

The winemaking vocabulary is quite expansive, and many terms are used interchangeably, often incorrectly, or are used differently by winemakers. Here you will find short definitions of many key words used in this book, as used by home winemakers. The terms are defined in greater detail in relevant chapters.

Wine is usually defined broadly as a fermented beverage from any raw material, such as grapes, fruit, vegetables and flowers, which contains primarily sugar but also starch. In this book, "wine" refers to fermented beverages made from grapes or grape derivatives, that is, fresh juice, sterile juice that has been processed to be shelf-stable, and concentrate.

Words in italics within definitions refer to terms defined elsewhere in this glossary.

A

Acetaldehyde: A volatile substance formed in small amounts by *yeast* metabolism during *alcoholic fermentation*. It is also formed by *oxidation* of *ethanol* and where it can impart a strong bruised-apple smell, a clear sign of advanced oxidative spoilage.

Acetic acid: A volatile acid with a distinct vinegar smell. It is the major acid in *volatile acidity (VA)*.

Acetobacter: Acetic acid bacteria responsible for *acetic acid* and *volatile acidity (VA)* in wine that has been overly exposed to oxygen.

Acidification: The process of adding one or more acids to increase the *acidity* of *must* or wine.

Acidity: The general term used to describe the tart, sour taste from the combined effects of all acids in wine. It also refers to *total acidity (TA)*, which is measured by simple laboratory analysis.

Additive: A substance, such as a *fining* agent or *sulfur dioxide (SO$_2$)*, added to *must* or wine, which remains in the wine. Compare to *processing aid.*

Aging: Bulk aging refers to the time spent by wine in carboys from the end of the *alcoholic fermentation* to bottling. Bottle aging refers to the time spent by wine in bottles until consumed. Aging potential is an estimate of how long a wine can be expected to age before its quality starts declining.

Airlock: A device used on a *carboy* to allow *carbon dioxide (CO$_2$)* gas to escape during fermentation and aging while keeping air (oxygen), dust and other elements out.

Alcoholic fermentation: The conversion of fermentable sugars—glucose and fructose—into alcohol (*ethanol*) and *carbon dioxide (CO$_2$)* gas by *yeast.*

Amelioration: The practice of adding water to *must* for the purpose of lowering the initial sugar level or acidity, i.e., *Specific Gravity (SG)* or *total acidity (TA)*, respectively.

Anthocyanins: The color pigment molecules, belonging to the broad class of compounds known as *polyphenols*, found in red grape skins and the pulp of certain varieties—called *teinturiers*—that give red and rosé wines their color.

Aromas: A term used here to describe all positive odors that can be smelled in wine, i.e., aromas from grapes, from *yeast* metabolism, and from *aging.*

Astringency: A tactile sensation of dryness and roughness on the palate caused by wine *tannins* binding with saliva proteins when we taste and drink red wine. Compare to *bitterness.*

Autolysis: The breakdown of dead *yeast* cells, or *lees*, as *alcoholic fermentation* nears completion.

B

Backsweeten: See *sweeten*.

Bacteria: Microorganisms mainly involved in spoilage, such as acetic acid bacteria responsible for producing *acetic acid* when, for example, wine is excessively exposed to oxygen. There are also beneficial bacteria, such as *malolactic bacteria* involved in *malolactic fermentation (MLF)*.

Balance: A descriptor for wine where *acidity*, sweetness and sugar, alcohol, and *tannins* coexist in harmony without any one element dominating.

Bench trials: Tests performed on a small scale with juice or wine samples to assess the qualitative or quantitative impacts of adding varying amounts of *additives* or *processing aids*, for example, to correct some deficiency. The amount determined that best achieves the desired results is then scaled up to treat an entire batch.

Bitterness: A term used to describe the bitter taste (as opposed to tactile sensation) of *tannins*. Compare to *astringency*.

Blend: A wine made up of two or more different wines, either from different grape varieties, from grapes of the same *variety* but sourced from different *vintages* or vineyards. Compare to *varietal*.

Body: A term that describes the "weight," "fullness" or "richness" of wine. Body depends mainly on alcohol content, *tannins*, *acidity*, *polysaccharides*, color and amount of *residual sugar (RS)*. A richly colored red wine with high alcohol and tannins is said to be full-bodied. Fruity, *dry* or *off-dry* white wines are said to be light-bodied. Compare to *structure*.

Bottle shock: Often used interchangeably with "bottle sickness," this refers to a temporary condition where a wine has seemingly become devoid of its wonderful pre-bottling *aromas* and flavors. It is believed to be the result of rapid *oxidation* during the bottling process that causes a small amount of *acetaldehyde* to form.

Brettanomyces (Brett): A term that refers to both the indigenous yeast and the flaw it creates in wine. It gives wine an unappealing barnyard smell, unappealing to those not partial to this odor.

Brewing: The production of beer by steeping, for example, malt, barley, or other sources of starch in water and then fermenting the liquid. This term is often used interchangeably, albeit incorrectly, with winemaking.

Bung: A rubber or silicone *carboy* stopper, either solid or with a hole to accommodate an *airlock*.

Cap: The mass of red grape solids that forms and floats to the top of a pail or vat as wine ferments. A cap signifies that *alcoholic fermentation* is well in progress with *carbon dioxide (CO$_2$)* gas pushing red grape solids to the surface.

Carbon dioxide (CO$_2$): A gas produced primarily during *alcoholic fermentation* but also during *malolactic fermentation (MLF)*.

Carboy: A glass or plastic container of standard size, mainly 5 and 6 gallons (19 and 23 liters). Also known as demijohn.

Chaptalization: The practice of adding sugar to juice or fermenting wine for the purpose of increasing *Potential Alcohol (PA)*.

Clarification: The process of clearing wine via natural *sedimentation*, the use of *fining* agents, or by *filtration*.

Cleaning: The process of removing dirt, debris and organic matter from processing equipment and tools in preparation for *sanitizing*.

Cold crashing: See *cold stabilization*. It can also be used to stop an active fermentation when natural residual sugar and sweetness are desired.

Cold settling: The technique of letting white or rosé juice settle at cold temperatures to allow *sedimentation* of grape fragments and other particulates that would otherwise interfere with *yeast* metabolism during *alcoholic fermentation*.

Cold stabilization: The process of chilling wine at cold temperatures—close to freezing—to force *tartrates* to form in bulk rather than forming later in bottles. Also referred to as *cold crashing* in home winemaking. See also *tartrate stabilization*.

Concentrate: Juice that has been processed to partially remove water and then stabilized and packaged into a kit or packaged in cans or bottles. To make wine, water is added to the concentrate and then fermented.

Conditioner: A sugary liquid product used to *sweeten* wine. It contains *sorbate* as a preservative to prevent refermentation.

Counterfining: The practice of adding a second *fining* agent to either improve the efficacy of the first fining agent or, for example, to help it settle once it has formed larger clusters so it can be completely removed by *racking*. It is also referred to as dual-stage fining.

Crushing: The process of gently splitting berries open to facilitate release of juice during *pressing* in white winemaking or to expose juice to grape solids during *maceration* in red winemaking.

D

Deacidification: The process of reducing one or more acids to lower the *acidity* of juice or wine.

Degassing: The process of removing *carbon dioxide (CO_2)* gas from wine prior to *clarification* and bottling, or from wine samples to be analyzed, for example, for *total acidity (TA)*.

Destemming: The process of removing stems from grape bunches before or after *crushing*, depending on equipment used. Stems can impart harsh, bitter *tannins*.

Dry: A wine is said to be "dry" when all fermentable sugars have been fermented, or when the wine has no perceptible sweetness, although it has some *residual sugar (RS)* but which has high *acidity*.

E

Enzymes: *Processing aids* that enable or facilitate reactions without themselves undergoing any change. These reactions could otherwise not happen or could take much longer to occur. For example, naturally occurring or added pectic enzymes, or pectinases, break down *pectin* transferred from skins into juice and improve *clarification* and *filtration*.

Ethanol: The major alcohol produced by *yeast* during *alcoholic fermentation*.

Ethyl acetate: A volatile substance with a sharp nail polish remover smell, the result of advanced *oxidation*.

F

Fault: A defect, such as oxidized wine or wine afflicted with *volatile acidity (VA)*, which adversely affects the taste or enjoyment of wine. Compare to *flaw*.

Fermentation: Refers to *alcoholic fermentation* when used without a qualifier.

Fermentor: A pail, vat or *carboy* used for fermenting wine.

Filtration: The process of clarifying wine by mechanical means through filter pads or cartridges.

Fining: Another term for *clarification*, but it also refers to the process of treating, for example, excessive *proteins*, harsh *tannins*, or poor color via the use of *additives* or *fining* agents. Compare to *clarification*.

Flaw: An abnormality or a distraction, but not quite a serious defect, which does not adversely affect the taste or enjoyment of wine. Compare to *fault*.

Free-run: The portion of juice or wine obtained by simple drainage of liquid, i.e., without *pressing* grape solids. Compare to *press-run*.

H

Headspace: The space above the surface of the wine in a wine bottle or *carboy*, which contains air and causes *oxidation* if not otherwise removed by vacuum or displaced with inert gas. Also referred to as ullage.

Heat stabilization: See *protein stabilization*.

Hybrids: Refers to grape varieties the result of interspecific crossing, i.e., crossing or hybridization of two species from the same genus. See also *native varieties*, *viniferas*.

Hydrogen sulfide (H_2S): A volatile sulfur compound with an unpleasant smell of rotten eggs, sewage or struck flint, often the result of leaving wine too long on the gross *lees*.

Hydrometer: An instrument used to measure *Specific Gravity (SG)* to estimate the amount of sugar in juice and therefore *Potential Alcohol (PA)*, and to monitor fermentation progress in wine.

I

Inoculation: The point at which *yeast* is added to juice or *must*, to initiate *alcoholic fermentation*, or *malolactic bacteria* are added to juice, *must* or wine, to initiate *malolactic fermentation (MLF)*.

Inoculum: The *yeast* or bacterium preparation for inoculating juice or *must*, to start *alcoholic fermentation* or *malolactic fermentation (MLF)*.

J

Juice: *Free-* and *press-run* juice obtained from crushing or pressing grapes. Once juice is ready to be fermented, it is referred to as *must*.

K

KMS: Short for *potassium metabisulfite*.

L

Lactic acid: An important wine acid resulting from the conversion of *malic acid* by *malolactic bacteria* during *malolactic fermentation (MLF)*.

Lactic acid bacteria: See *malolactic bacteria*.

Lees: Sediment that forms at the bottom of a pail or *carboy*, mainly during *alcoholic fermentation*, which is referred to as "gross lees," but which also forms during *aging* and is then referred to as "fine lees." Lees contain dead *yeast* cells, grape solid fragments, *tartrates*, *polysaccharides*, *bacteria* and other precipitable matter.

M

Maceration: The red winemaking technique of macerating, or "steeping," grape skins in juice for the purpose of extracting *aromas*, flavors, color and *tannins*.

Malic acid: The second most significant acid, after *tartaric acid*, found in grapes. In reds, it is most often converted into *lactic acid* by *malolactic bacteria* during *malolactic fermentation (MLF)*.

Malolactic bacteria: Also referred to as lactic acid bacteria, the bacteria responsible for *malolactic fermentation (MLF)*.

Malolactic fermentation (MLF): The enzymatic conversion of the sharper-tasting *malic acid* into the softer *lactic acid* by *malolactic bacteria* for the purpose of reducing *acidity* as well as to add *aromas* and flavors.

Mercaptans: An old term still in use to refer to a class of foul-smelling sulfur compounds, such as *hydrogen sulfide (H_2S)*, resulting primarily from post-fermentation interactions between gross *lees* and sulfur compounds.

Microbial spoilage: Any kind of spoilage of microbial nature, i.e., caused by microorganisms, such as *yeast* and *bacteria*.

Microbial stability: The state of wine when it is protected against microorganisms that could otherwise cause *microbial spoilage*. Microbial stability can be achieved by adding a preservative, such as *sulfur dioxide (SO_2)*.

Micron: Short for micrometer, the unit of measure of filter media porosity.

Mouthfeel: A term used in conjunction with "body" to describe the tactile sensation felt on the palate and in the mouth due to *tannins*, alcohol, *polysaccharides* and *residual sugar (RS)*. Compare to *body*.

Must: The material that gets fermented, that is, juice in making white or rosé wine, or juice and all its dissolved solids as well as crushed grapes in making red wine. Once fermentation has started and alcohol is being produced, it is then referred to as *wine*.

Mycoderma: A spoilage condition caused by aerobic surface yeast, called *Candida mycoderma*, which creates a whitish film floating and expanding on the surface of wine that is overly exposed to oxygen.

Native varieties: Refers to grape varieties indigenous to a specific grape-growing region. See also *hybrids*, *viniferas*.

Nutrients: Naturally occurring nitrogen-containing substances used by *yeast* and *bacteria* to successfully carry out their metabolic functions during *alcoholic fermentation* and *malolactic fermentation (MLF)*. *Musts* are often deficient in nutrients and must be supplemented with *additives*.

Off-dry: A wine is said to be off-dry when it has a hint or more of perceptible sweetness.

Oxidation: A spoilage condition arising from excessive exposure to oxygen. It can cause wine to turn to a darkish orange color and then brown, it can mute *aromas*, and it can cause the conversion of compounds into undesirable substances, for example, *ethanol* into *acetaldehyde*.

P

Pearson Square: A simple visual formula to calculate the proportions of two juices or wines needed to create a blend with a desired concentration of, for example, *total acidity (TA)* or alcohol.

Pectin: A class of substances, or *polysaccharides*, found in the cell walls of grape skins, which can cause problems with *clarification* and *filtration* if not broken down by pectic *enzymes* (pectinases).

pH: A measure of the strength of acids in juice or wine. Compare to *total acidity (TA)*.

Polyphenols: A very broad class of compounds that includes *tannins* and *anthocyanins*. The word is often used interchangeably with "phenolics" for brevity.

Polysaccharides: Long chains of many monosaccharides, such as simple sugar molecules. *Yeast* polysaccharides contribute to *body* by giving a sense of "fullness" on the palate.

Pomace: The mass of grape solids either from *pressing* grapes in white winemaking or pressing crushed grapes that have macerated in wine in red winemaking. Also referred to as "cake."

Potassium: A naturally occurring mineral (as K^+ ions) found in grapes and translocated to wine and which can be a source of high *pH* or cause *tartrates* to form when wine is subjected to cold temperatures.

Potassium bitartrate: The chemical name for *tartrates*, the salt crystals that form and precipitate from *potassium* and *tartaric acid* when wine is subjected to cold temperatures.

Potassium metabisulfite: The potassium salt of metabisulfite used in winemaking; it is used for *sanitizing* equipment and also as a preservative against *oxidation* and *microbial spoilage*. It is often referred to simply as *sulfite* or "KMS," the "K" being the element symbol for *potassium*.

Potential Alcohol (PA): The predicted maximum amount of alcohol (*ethanol*) that can potentially be produced if *yeast* converts all fermentable sugars during *alcoholic fermentation*.

Pressing: The process of pressing grape solids to extract juice in white and rosé winemaking or to extract wine following *maceration* and *alcoholic fermentation* in red winemaking.

Press-run: The portion of juice or wine obtained by *pressing* grape solids. Compare to *free-run*.

Primary fermentation: A term used by amateur winemakers; it refers to the vigorous phase of *alcoholic fermentation*. Once transferred to a *carboy* (see *racking*), the continuation of the *alcoholic fermentation* is referred to as *secondary fermentation*.

Processing aid: An *additive* used, for example, to clarify wine or precipitate harsh *tannins*, but which itself becomes removed following *racking*. Compare to *additive*.

Proteins: Very large molecules consisting of long chains of amino acids. Proteins can be a source of cloudiness, or protein haze, in white and rosé wines, especially when subjected to warmer temperatures, and must therefore be removed by *fining*.

Protein stabilization: Also known as heat stabilization, the process of adding a suitable *fining* agent, such as bentonite, to remove *proteins* in juice or wine that could otherwise cause cloudiness or a haze.

Punchdown: The red winemaking technique of "punching down" the *cap* into the *must* or wine by mechanical means during *maceration* and fermentation to favor extraction of *polyphenols*, homogenize temperature, and protect against *microbial spoilage*.

Pyrazines: A class of compounds found in Cabernet-related varieties which impart a vegetal, green bell pepper character to wine, especially when made from underripe fruit.

Racking: The process of transferring juice or wine from one vessel to another by gravity or using a pump for the purpose of separating the liquid from a layer of sediment.

Reduction: The opposite of *oxidation*; a condition that gives rise to sulfur compounds, such as *hydrogen sulfide (H_2S)*, in the absence of oxygen.

Residual sugar (RS): The portion of natural sugars remaining in wine after completion of the *alcoholic fermentation*, plus any sugars added to *sweeten* wine. See *body* and *mouthfeel*.

Rice hulls: Hulls or husks of rice used as *pressing* aids, particularly useful when dealing with slipskin grape varieties, to facilitate the flow of juice or wine through the *pomace* in the press.

Rosé: French for "pink"; refers to any pink-colored wine.

S

Sanitizing: The process of removing and inhibiting microorganisms from winemaking equipment down to a level deemed to pose no risk of spoilage. *Cleaning* is a necessary step before sanitizing.

Secondary fermentation: A term used by amateur winemakers which refers to the less vigorous phase of *alcoholic fermentation* following *primary fermentation*.

Sedimentation: The natural, physical process whereby suspended, insoluble matter in juice or wine precipitates and settles to the bottom of a pail or *carboy*.

SO_2: See *sulfur dioxide (SO_2)*.

Sorbate: A preservative to prevent refermentation in wine with residual natural or added fermentable sugars.

Specific Gravity (SG): A measure of the estimated amount of sugars in juice to estimate the *Potential Alcohol (PA)*, and to monitor the progress of *alcoholic fermentation*.

Stabilization: Refers to any of the various processes used to protect wine against, for example, *oxidation*, *microbial spoilage* or the formation of *tartrates*.

Sterile juice: Juice for making wine and which has been processed to be shelf-stable, i.e., it does not require refrigeration.

Structure: A term often used in conjunction with, or often interchangeably with "body", to describe the taste and sensation of wine. Both "structure" and "body" may refer more specifically to the relationship between *tannins* and *acidity* without considering alcohol and *polysaccharides*. Compare to *body*.

Sulfite: The short name for any of the sulfite salts (e.g., *potassium metabisulfite*, sodium metabisulfite) used as preservatives in wine. It is commonly used interchangeably with *sulfur dioxide (SO₂)*.

Sulfur dioxide (SO₂): A gas, which, when dissolved in wine, acts as a preservative and protects against *microbial spoilage* and *oxidation*. SO_2 is added to wine most commonly using a *sulfite* salt, usually *potassium metabisulfite*.

Sweeten: The practice of adding sugar, juice *concentrate*, wine *conditioner*, or other sweetening agent to a finished wine for a sweeter style or for offsetting high *acidity*. Often referred to as "backsweeten."

T

Tannins: A broad subclass of *polyphenols* found in grape skins, seeds, stems and oak wood, which are in part responsible for *body* and *structure* in wine, particularly reds. Tannins are also very good antioxidants.

Tartaric acid: The most important acid in grapes and wine. It is also a source of *tartrates*.

Tartrates: The common word for *potassium bitartrate* salt crystals. Also known as "wine diamonds" and cream of tartar.

Tartrate stabilization: A process involving adding an inhibitor, an *additive*, or subjecting wine to cold temperatures to avoid *tartrates* from forming later in bottles. Compare to *cold stabilization*.

TCA: Short for 2,4,6-trichloroanisole, the substance responsible for cork taint in so-called "corked wine." It imparts a moldy, musty smell to wine.

Teinturier: French for "dyer." A word used to refer to any red grape *variety* that has red skin but also red juice and pulp, i.e., it can make red wine without *maceration*. Teinturier varieties are often used as blending wines to improve color in deficient reds or for making *rosé*.

Titration: An analytical method used to determine the concentration of specific substances, such as acids, in juice or wine. See *total acidity (TA)*.

Topping: The practice of adding wine to a *carboy* to minimize *headspace* and thereby reduce the risks of *oxidation* or *microbial spoilage*.

Total acidity (TA): A measurement of the concentration of acids in juice and wine; it is determined by *titration*. Compare to *pH*.

U

Ullage: See *headspace*.

V

Varietal: Refers to wine made from a single *variety*; for example, a wine made from 100% Chardonnay grapes is a varietal. Compare to *variety*. Compare to *blend*.

Variety: Refers to "grape variety"; for example, Cabernet Sauvignon is a grape variety. Compare to *varietal*. See *hybrids*; *viniferas*.

Viniferas: Refers to grape varieties native to the Mediterranean region, Central Europe, and southwestern Asia. Often simply referred to as European varieties. See also *hybrids*, *native varieties*.

Vintage: The year grapes were grown.

Volatile acidity (VA): Consists primarily of *acetic acid*, an acid produced in tiny amounts by *yeast* during *alcoholic fermentation* and which adds aromatic complexity to wine; however, when detected as a distinct vinegar smell, it is considered a *fault*. In the presence of oxygen, it can be produced by *Acetobacter bacteria*, as in the making of vinegar, or in poorly topped up carboys.

W

Wine: In this guide, "wine" refers to fermented beverages made from grapes or grape derivatives (e.g., fresh juice, *sterile juice*, or *concentrate*). Compare to *brewing*.

Y

Yeast: In winemaking, "yeast" refers primarily to *Saccharomyces cerevisiae* yeast, the microorganism responsible for metabolizing sugar into *ethanol* and the numerous other by-products that give wines their many *aromas* and flavors.

Yield: The expected or actual volume of juice, raw wine or finished wine that a certain quantity of grapes will provide.

CHAPTER ONE

Introduction

*T*his beginner's guide is for those who want to take up this fun hobby and start making wine at home from juice or grapes—great wine that you can proudly call your own.

This guide teaches you the fundamentals of winemaking and walks you through the process in very practical terms, from processing grapes to fermenting juice and readying wine for bottling. It's not a recipe book. But there are specific chapters with step-by-step instructions for making white, rosé, and red wine from juice or grapes, including a comprehensive troubleshooting guide for when something does not go quite as expected or when you run into a problem.

You'll need to learn only some basic wine science: that is, what are specific gravity, acidity, and pH and how to measure these not only for making great wine but for doing so consistently. Sulfur dioxide (SO_2), too, is important, albeit a more advanced subject. You won't need to understand the science of SO_2 here, but you'll still find specific instructions on how and when to add sulfite, if you so choose, to protect your wine from spoilage.

As you gain experience and confidence and want to explore more advanced winemaking, wine analysis, and troubleshooting techniques, and perhaps learn some of the wine chemistry behind it all, you can consult my book *Modern Home Winemaking: A Guide to Making Consistently Great Wines* (Véhicule Press, 2021). You'll also find additional information and downloadable tools on my website, ModernHomeWinemaking.com, to help you with various winemaking calculations.

ABOUT BATCH SIZES

There are two standard batch sizes in home winemaking: a 5-gallon (19-liter) carboy and a 6-gallon (23-liter) carboy. The former is more common, and therefore, all instructions and additives presented here are for making 5-gal (19-L) batches. Since you'll need to ferment in a larger carboy and you'll also "lose" some wine during various operations that require you to top up a carboy, you'll need to start with a 6-gal (23-L) carboy to finish with 5 gal (19 L) of wine in a 5-gal carboy ... and perhaps a touch more. You'll find in Chapter SIX (pp. 102–103) a description of how to manage these volumes. You can easily scale up these volumes and instructions as you grow your hobby.

THE PASSION OF HOME WINEMAKING

I remember, when I was a very young kid, how my Italian parents, who had lived through the Second World War, would make their own prosciutto, *lonza* and other *salumi* (cured meat), *salsiccia* (Italian sausage), and fresh, handmade pasta and would grow their own vegetables in their small backyard garden. And, of course, my dad made his own wine. They had learned and grown up to be self-sufficient, to do as much as possible themselves.

Of these traditions, winemaking is the main one I have carried forward since my childhood. I was always fascinated by the process of crushing grapes. Come fall, I would get all excited when my dad would go to the local market and bring back a truckload of Alicante. It was almost always Alicante Bouschet. I would insist on working the crusher—the manual kind, of course—and lament the blisters the next morning. There was something special and magical about the whole process, because I didn't understand how grapes transformed into this mysterious beverage called wine. My dad would simply say, "*Lascialo bollire,*" just "let it boil," his generation's layman's way of saying, "Let it ferment." And he added nothing, "*ma no,*" no additives or preservatives. Fermentation would last seven days on average, perhaps a few more in our unheated garage if we had a cold fall. Soon, in the new year, he would transfer the wine to another vessel, but never on a full-moon night, then "bottle" it in one-gallon jugs. Jugs were the most practical. Bottles would not last long and were deemed too impractical. Wine was a daily beverage that accompanied every meal, and not a weekend would go by without all the *paesans* getting together every Saturday night to enjoy food and wine.

As I grew up and became passionate about the physical sciences, I learned everything I could about winemaking, greatly influenced by my Italian enologist cousin, Giacomo Cocci, who would later refer to me as "the student that teaches the teacher." But my greatest honor was when my dad asked me to make his wine—to take over. It was his way of saying, "You make some darn good wine."

And so it is that I continue this tradition, not out of necessity or a need for self-sufficiency but for the joy of creating my own wines. But, as some would say, this passion has evolved into an obsession. Understanding wine, including wine chemistry, is all a part of the challenge of making better and greater wine. As you get into home winemaking, whether to continue a family tradition or to craft your own for pleasure, the hobby will soon grow into a passion. Your production, too, will grow as you'll soon want to experiment with different grape varieties and wine styles.

CAN I MAKE NATURAL WINES—WITHOUT ANY ADDITIVES OR PRESERVATIVES?

There is no clear definition, or at least not a universally accepted one, for "natural wine," but it generally means wine made without the use of additives or processing aids and, to many wine enthusiasts, without any kind of intervention or mechanical treatment such as filtration. Those growing grapes extend the definition to mean that the grapes used are grown organically, without the use of pesticides or other vineyard chemicals.

You'll notice throughout that I deliberately differentiate between additives and processing aids.

An additive is any ingredient that remains in the wine or which is consumed or transformed over time. Sulfite (a widely used preservative) and yeast nutrients are examples of additives. Purists who rely on indigenous yeast to ferment juice consider commercial yeast, too, as an additive.

A processing aid is a substance that, when added to wine, slowly precipitates to the bottom of the carboy and is removed when wine is racked to another carboy. Racking means to transfer wine from one carboy to another to separate it from the layer of sediment to be discarded. Bentonite, a type of clay, and chitosan, a polysaccharide derived from crustaceans, both used for clarifying wine, are examples of processing aids. In theory, there should be no processing aid left in the wine, although there could potentially be trace amounts, and this may be significant to those who have specific allergies. Some vegans may be opposed to any use of non-vegan processing aids, whether or not they remain in the wine.

The use of additives, processing aids, and mechanical treatments is an approach sometimes perceived as too interventionist, unnecessary, harmful, or not traditional (although reasons why the last is so important are not clear), and patience is seen as the only ingredient you need to make great wine. Setting our personal beliefs aside, is it possible to make natural wine without the use of these?

The short answer is yes: yes, you can make wine—very good wine—by fermenting it with indigenous yeast, letting it clarify to a perfectly clear appearance on its own, without using preservatives. But things don't always go as expected. You don't know how the indigenous yeast will interact with that load of grapes just delivered to your garage. It can give off odors and flavors and perhaps cause fermentation problems. Moreover, you don't know if there might be a nutrient deficiency that will cause undue stress on the yeast. And what if a wine stubbornly refuses to clear on its own? Or you have to deal with a wine with very low acidity? Or, perhaps, what if it has residual sugar that may cause spontaneous fermentation in bottles? What if you want to lay away your finest wine and age it for a few years? Can this be done without preservatives?

My winemaking is driven by an intimate knowledge of wine science. My decisions to use additives and processing aids and to filter wine are all based on an assessment of impacts from a scientific viewpoint. This guide reflects my experience and the application of modern knowledge and techniques to what I call "modern home winemaking." This is what allows me to craft very good wines consistently while eliminating, to the extent possible, any risk of problems during the journey from grapes to bottle. As you gain experience and become more comfortable with the use of additives and modern techniques, you'll develop your own ways (and opinions) that best suit your preferences and styles of wine.

HOW SHOULD I START: KIT, JUICE, OR GRAPES?

If you have never made wine, start out with a kit (Figure 1.1); it's a great way to learn the process as well as why you need to do what's instructed. Make several batches until you become comfortable with the process. Kits require minimal equipment and space and come with all the necessary ingredients to make very good wine in a foolproof way in less than a couple of months any time of the year. You simply add water to the concentrated juice, then you follow the instructions step by step. There have been tremendous improvements since the kits of yesteryear. You can now find premium wine kits with 100% juice needing no water—also with grape skins for adding more body to your liking and in many styles from many grape varieties. All the concepts described in this guide also apply to kit winemaking, unless otherwise stated; you can also consult my book *Kit Winemaking: The Illustrated Beginner's Guide to Making Wine from Concentrate* (Véhicule Press, 2009).

Figure 1.1: A six-week wine kit

From kit wines, you can grow into making wine using fresh (refrigerated) or frozen juice if you want more control and would like to decide every step of the way how to process the juice into wine according to your preferences. Fresh and frozen juices are sold in 5-, 5.3-, and 6-gal (19-, 20-, and 23-L) pails and are usually available only in the fall in North America (or the northern hemisphere), or perhaps even in the spring if you can find a supplier of southern-hemisphere juice from Chile, Argentina, or South Africa. But, in this case, you have to know the supplier and their products so you understand if and how the juice was processed. Some will adjust sugar, acidity, and pH levels so that you don't need to worry about making adjustments to craft a balanced wine. We'll talk about balance below. You'll also need to know if any sulfite was added, and how much, because, naturalness and tradition aside, you may not be able to put the wine through malolactic fermentation (MLF) if that is your intent. *Malo-what?* It's an additional fermentation used to smoothen acidity. We'll tackle this topic in Chapter SEVEN.

Some vendors offer frozen red must—that is, juice with crushed, destemmed grapes for making red wine. This is an excellent option not only because it saves you from having to crush and destem grapes but also because the freezing–thawing cycle further breaks down grape skins and causes them to release more color.

You'll also find sterile, shelf-stable juice sold in 5-gal (19-L) pails that you can buy to make wine any time of the year. As with concentrate in kits, the juice is pasteurized and stabilized to prevent spontaneous fermentation, and it is also balanced for sugar, acidity, and pH. You may have to buy some ingredients separately.

And then, of course, you can make wine from grapes. You can buy grapes most commonly in 36-lb (16.4-kg) crates, sometimes 18-lb (8.2-kg) lugs, or in bulk directly from a vineyard. You'll need to invest in the necessary equipment to crush and press grapes. You'll need more space, and this route is messier, but you'll have total control over how to process the grapes, including how much color and tannins to extract when making reds. But be ready for some challenges. More often than not, you'll be faced with too little or too much sugar or acidity, or pH that is too high, and you'll need to make quick decisions on adjustments to be able to produce a balanced wine. It's not always easy or straightforward. Some knowledge of wine science will be an asset.

And if you're interested in making fruit and country wines—that is, wines made from fruit other than grapes or from vegetables, flowers, or herbs—you'll find many recipes and lots of great advice in Jack Keller's book *Home Winemaking: The Simple Way to Make Delicious Wine* (Adventure Publications, 2021).

ABOUT ALCOHOL, ACIDITY, SWEETNESS, AND TANNINS

Wine should be balanced to be most enjoyable.

Okay. What does that mean?

Alcohol, acidity, sweetness, and tannins are the four pillars of wine balance. If any of these is too low or excessive, the wine is out of balance and not at its best, perhaps not very enjoyable.

In general, compared to reds, white wines have lower alcohol, in the 11%–13% range; higher acidity, perhaps bone dry or slightly sweet; and no tannins. Whites are usually served colder to bring acidity to life, to make the wine taste more refreshing. And some sweetness can offset high acidity, where it works well with certain styles of wines. Most whites are meant for quick consumption, usually within 12 months or so of production. Of course, there are exceptions, as there are many, many other styles of whites, such as full-bodied, oak barrel-aged Chardonnays with their lower acidity and with tannins transferred from barrel wood that give them more character as well as longer aging potential.

Reds, on the other hand, have higher alcohol, in the 13%–15% range; lower acidity, usually dry with no sweetness; and lots of tannins to give them more body and structure as well as greater mouthfeel. Tannins and their antioxidant properties are what give reds their longer aging potential. Acidity can make tannins unpleasantly harsh on the palate. That's why reds have lower acidity. On the other hand, tannins allow for higher alcohol and therefore more body.

Rosé wines are kind of in between, still looking to carve out an identity with consumers. Some styles will drink more like a white and have higher acidity, served chilled, and some will lean more toward a red style with lower acidity and some tannins.

The concepts are straightforward, the winemaking not always so. Sometimes you'll be faced with less than perfectly balanced juice from poorly grown fruit or from over-cropping; maybe from fruit of a poor vintage because of a rainy, cold growing season; or from blemished or moldy fruit damaged during transportation. You may need to add sugar to get to your desired alcohol range, or add water—*argh!*—to bring down what will be excessive alcohol, or perhaps boost acidity if it's too low or when faced with high pH (which increases the risk of microbial spoilage). It can often be a challenge not to intervene to make the necessary adjustments.

WHAT ARE THE BEST GRAPE VARIETIES FOR MAKING WINE?

There are many, many grape varieties from which to choose to make white, rosé, and red wine, and which can be made in varied styles, from dry to sweet. You'll only be limited by what you're able to source. But be sure to choose grapes that can make great wine, which is what we're after. Table grapes, meant for consumption as fruit, don't make good wine, as they don't have enough sugars and tend to lack acidity.

The most common grape varieties for making wine are so-called European varieties, known as viniferas. These include the likes of Chardonnay, Moscato, Riesling, and Sauvignon Blanc in whites, and Aglianico, Cabernet Sauvignon, Petite Sirah, Pinot Noir, and Zinfandel in reds.

And then there are many, many native varieties and hybrids. Native varieties are those indigenous to a specific grape-growing region. Scuppernong and Concord are examples of Native American varieties. Hybrids result from the crossing of two or more varieties from different species in the genus *Vitis*. They are created to take advantage of the best characteristics of the crossed varieties and, ideally, to eliminate their weaknesses: for example, to improve their winter hardiness or their resistance to specific diseases. American hybrids result from the crossing of varieties from Native American species. French–American hybrids, such as Baco Noir, result from the crossing of varieties from vinifera and American species.

The best way to learn about grape varieties and wine styles is to learn the characteristics of each variety and the styles it best creates (and why) and to taste lots of different wines. You'll come to develop a preference for certain varieties and styles, and those should guide you in your home winemaking. Make wine that you like: to please your palate—and your family's too, of course.

You can learn about popular grape varieties in my book *Modern Home Winemaking*; or by doing an online search; or by consulting the most authoritative book, *Wine Grapes: A Complete Guide to 1,368 Vine Varieties, Including Their Origins and Flavours*, co-authored by Jancis Robinson, Julia Harding, and José Vouillamoz (Ecco Press, 2012).

HOW WINE IS MADE: AN OVERVIEW

The following overview of how each type of wine—white, rosé, and red— is made will help you understand the relevance and importance of each process or step and the use of additives and processing aids. You'll find step-by-step instructions for making each type in Chapters FOURTEEN, FIFTEEN, and SIXTEEN, respectively. The context here is small-scale home winemaking and standard carboy-sized batches without the use of oak barrels or stainless steel tanks. When you are ready to invest in and make use of oak barrels and stainless steel tanks, consult my book *Techniques in Home Winemaking: The Comprehensive Guide to Making Château-Style Wines* (Véhicule Press, 2008) for more information.

In all the processes described below, grapes are always destemmed, meaning stems are removed, when they are crushed. Stem tannins can impart a bitter taste and harsh sensation.

To make great wines consistently, you have to manage the process diligently and with great patience, without rushing. Keep meticulous records of all activities and measurements, additives and processing aids used, as well as tasting notes. Not only will you have a documented history of your process, which you can consult to reliably replicate a specific style, but you'll also have all the detailed data to perform a root-cause analysis if you run into a problem. You can download a log sheet for record keeping at ModernHomeWinemaking.com.

And a word about entering wine into amateur competitions, as you'll surely soon want to do. First make sure you are able to objectively assess your wine with a critical palate and nose so you are not submitting flawed (or spoiled) wine. Have friends and family—those whose palate you trust—taste your wines and then enter only those you feel are your best. Don't rush into submitting wines prematurely, and certainly don't rush through the winemaking process.

White Winemaking

White is the easiest of the three wines to make, but it is also the most fragile, because it is susceptible to spoilage if overly exposed to oxygen. It must be protected as much as possible from the elements, from grapes to bottle.

Grapes are crushed and destemmed, then pressed, or possibly just pressed as whole clusters without crushing, to extract the juice. A short maceration of grape skins in juice before pressing can add aromas and flavors. Maceration means letting the crushed grapes soak for a short time before pressing. The pressed juice is chilled, or cold settled, to inhibit spontaneous fermentation while heavy solids and particulates settle to the bottom of the pail or carboy. The partially cleared juice is then racked or separated from the thick sediment layer. At this point, the juice is referred to as "must." The must is warmed up slightly to kickstart the alcoholic fermentation, either spontaneously, relying on indigenous yeast, or by adding cultured yeast.

Fermentation is carried out in a food-grade pail with a loosely placed lid or in a carboy completely protected from air and the elements. Except for very few grape varieties, most whites are not put through MLF to preserve the fruity style and all the acidity that gives whites their freshness. As we'll learn, MLF converts one type of acid into another to soften the wine's acidity. Fermentation can take a week or 10 days if done warm, and considerably longer at cooler temperatures to retain more of the delicate aromas and flavors.

Once fermentation is complete, wine is clarified, stabilized with sulfite to protect it from spoilage microorganisms, and stabilized against proteins that can cause haze as well as against tartrate crystals that may form if wine is subjected to cold temperatures. A fining agent—most commonly, bentonite—is used to remove those proteins, which will not immediately precipitate on their own into the sediment layer that will be racked from the bottom of the vessel. The wine is racked to separate out the sediment, with optional filtering to get a crystal-clear wine, and then bottled.

Rosé Winemaking

Making rosé wine will usually involve a short maceration to extract the desired amount of color from grape skins, but the juice and wine are then processed as in the making of white wine. Rosé wine, too, can be fragile and susceptible to oxidation, and so it must likewise be protected from the elements.

Grapes are first crushed and destemmed into a small vat and the grape solids allowed to macerate with the juice for a short period, from a couple to several hours or more depending on the grape variety and desired color. When the desired color is achieved, the mass of crushed grapes is pressed and the juice is transferred to a food-grade pail or carboy. Richly colored varieties, such as Syrah, are whole-cluster pressed—that is, without crushing—since too much color would be extracted otherwise.

The pressed, cold-settled juice, or must, is then processed as in the making of white wine.

Red Winemaking

Making red wine requires more work and is often a greater challenge as you try and extract as much color as desired while limiting the extraction of tannins to achieve your desired style. In the early stages of the process, reds actually need oxygen to maintain their vibrant, intense purplish red color. You'll often hear the term anthocyanins when discussing color: this is the chemical name for the red pigment molecules responsible for color in rosés and reds.

Grapes are crushed and destemmed into an open vat or similar vessel to allow the grape solids to macerate with the juice for the duration of fermentation. Enzymes and tannins are added right at crush to help extract and stabilize color. The mass of grape solids and juice is referred to as must at this point.

The must is then fermented, either spontaneously, relying on indigenous yeast, or by adding cultured yeast. Fermentation is carried out in an open vessel—for example, a food-grade plastic vat. Color and tannins are extracted from the grape solids during maceration and fermentation, with greater extraction at higher temperatures; color is extracted mostly early on in the first couple of days, while tannins are progressively extracted throughout as the alcohol increases.

As fermentation begins and starts producing lots of carbon dioxide (CO_2) gas, grape solids rise to the surface above the wine and create a mass referred to as cap. Two to three times daily, the cap is pushed and re-submerged into the fermenting wine—a technique known as "doing punchdowns"—to help extract color and tannins, to homogenize temperature to ensure good fermentation dynamics, and to keep spoilage microorganisms in check. Fermentation generally lasts 5 to 7 days, but it can be made to last longer depending on the desired style.

Once fermentation is complete, free-run wine (that portion which flows without pressing) is transferred to a carboy. Grape solids are pressed, and press-run wine is transferred to the same carboy or a different one to treat it separately. Press-run wine may be of lesser quality, which is why it is often treated separately.

Almost all reds are put through MLF to reduce acidity, to increase aroma and flavor complexities, and to improve microbial stability.

Following the completion of both fermentations, the wine is stabilized with sulfite to keep spoilage microorganisms in check.

Wine can be left to age in a glass or PET plastic carboy with or without oak chips or sticks, depending on the desired style. The wine is racked to separate out the sediment, with optional filtering for extra clarity, and then bottled.

CHAPTER TWO

What Equipment Do I Need?

*A*s you begin your journey into making wine, you'll need some basic equipment, and that may be all if you'll be making a single batch at a time from juice. If you want to make wine from grapes, then you'll need to invest in the equipment to crush and press grapes. Once you decide to scale up your production, consider upgrading with tools that will greatly simplify your winemaking.

THE ESSENTIALS

To make a standard batch of wine using juice or concentrate from a kit, you really only need some very basic, inexpensive equipment. Home wine-making supply shops sell a basic starter kit (Figure 2.1) that may include the following:

- **7.9-gal (30-L) food-grade pail** and **lid** for fermenting juice with or without grape solids. This is commonly referred to as a *primary fermentor* in home winemaking. The pail should be of food-grade HDPE (plastic code 02).

- **6-gal (23-L) carboy** (also known as *demijohn*) as a primary fermentor and **5-gal (19-L) carboy** as a *secondary fermentor* for completing fermentation and for storing and aging wine. Carboys can be of glass or PET (plastic code 01).

Figure 2.1: Basic winemaking starter kit

The section CONDUCTING AND MONITORING FERMENTA-TION in Chapter SIX defines *primary* and *secondary fermentation* in more detail and describes the use of primary and secondary fermentors.

You'll be doing a lot of transferring of wine (what is referred to as *racking*) from one container to another to separate wine from the sediment that forms at the bottom. An **extra 5-gal (19-L) carboy** will come in handy; otherwise, you'll have to transfer the wine, for example, from the carboy into the pail and back into the carboy. A second carboy not only eliminates this extra step, it also reduces exposure to air and contaminants that can compromise the quality of your wine.

And as you'll likely be moving glass carboys around, install **carrying handles**, use **carrier straps**, or best yet, place carboys in **heavy-duty plastic milk crates** (Figure 2.2) to avoid accidentally dropping a carboy. You can buy these crates from any big-box hardware store. Be sure to always use both hands when lifting a carboy, full or empty.

- **Triple-scale hydrometer** and **test cylinder** to measure the amount of sugar in juice and estimate potential alcohol that will be pro-

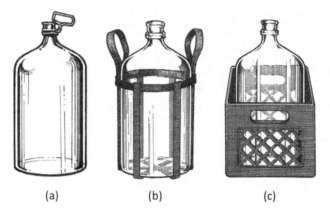

Figure 2.2: a) Carboy handle; b) carboy carrier strap; and c) carboy in milk crate

duced from the fermentation, and to monitor fermentation progress. Triple-scale means that the hydrometer measures the amount of sugar using three scales: Specific Gravity (SG), °Brix units, and Potential Alcohol (PA). These measurements are described in Chapter FIVE.

Buy an extra hydrometer for backup; sooner or later, you'll likely break one, and you don't want to be caught actively fermenting without measuring sugar consumption progress. Alternatively, look for one made of rugged plastic, such as the Herculometer, which won't break as glass hydrometers do.

- **Airlock** and **no. 7 bung** (stopper). An airlock is a one-way valve that allows gas generated during fermentation to escape out of the carboy and which also protects wine from impurities in the surrounding air. The most common types are the S-type and 3-piece wet airlocks (Figure 2.3) with a no. 7 rubber or silicone bung. Airlocks are filled with a sulfite solution or even vodka to form a barrier between wine and the external environment.

Figure 2.3: a) S-type wet airlock; b) 3-piece wet airlock

- ⅜-inch **racking cane** with an **anti-dregs tip** plus a **siphon hose** with a **flow-control clamp** (Figure 2.1) for racking wine from one fermentor to another. The anti-dregs tip avoids sucking up sediment during racking when done carefully.

Unless you'll be using a pump to transfer wine, you'll likely do it by siphoning. That means you'll be sucking on the siphon hose to start the flow of wine. If you don't fancy that idea, you can instead buy an **auto-siphon racking cane** (Figure 2.4) that you can manually pump to prime and start the flow of wine.

- **Long mixing spoon** (Figure 2.1) for stirring wine, for example, to introduce an additive or to degas (to remove carbon dioxide gas). Chapter EIGHT describes how to degas wine with a long mixing spoon and other types of devices.

Figure 2.4: Auto-siphon racking cane

You should also have on hand one or two **half-gallon** and **one-gallon jugs** as you'll often end up with a bit of extra wine that you'll need to manage and store separately.

Some vendors include some extra equipment and supplies (Figure 2.5) with their starter kits, such as:

- **Wine thief**, a device for drawing wine samples from fermentors for tasting and testing; an ordinary **kitchen baster** will work great too.

- **Floating thermometer** for monitoring fermentation temperature.

- Simple **wand-type bottle filler**.

- **Double-lever hand corker** for inserting corks into bottles.

- **Corks, capsules** and **labels**.

- **Cleaner** and **sanitizer** for cleaning and sanitizing equipment, tools, and bottles.

You'll need to buy separately **bottle-washing** and **sanitizing equipment**; we'll look at that equipment in Chapter THIRTEEN.

Carboys will get dirty from fermentation residues or become stained when making red wine. You'll need a soft-bristle, non-abrasive **brush** or **carboy cleaner** (Figure 2.6a) for removing those stubborn stains. A **carboy drainer** (Figure 2.6b) too will come in handy for drip-drying after a water rinse.

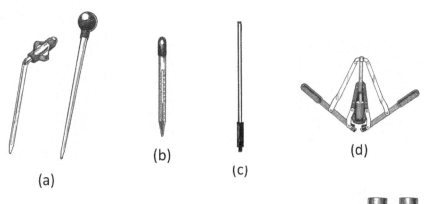

Figure 2.5: Other essential equipment and supplies: a) wine thief and kitchen baster; b) floating thermometer; c) wand-type bottle filler; d) double-lever hand corker; e) corks, capsules, labels; and f) cleaner and sanitizer

 Never use a brush or other cleaning device that has a metal component to clean glass carboys. The slightest contact between metal and glass can cause the carboy to shatter and cause serious injury.

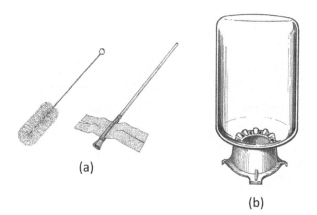

Figure 2.6: a) carboy brush and cleaner; b) carboy drainer

For pails and anything made of plastic, a soft, non-abrasive standard or foam-type sponge is best. A scratched surface will be very difficult to clean and sanitize and becomes a perfect breeding ground for spoilage microorganisms.

A **spray bottle** (Figure 2.7) for spraying equipment and tools with a sanitizing solution is also handy. You'll learn all about cleaning and sanitizing in Chapter THREE.

You'll be measuring a lot of additives, so you'll need a **measuring teaspoon (tsp)** and **tablespoon (tbsp)**, equivalent to 5 mL and 15 mL, respectively. For dry additives, a tsp is roughly 5 grams and a tbsp about 15 g. As additives

Figure 2.7: Spray bottle

have different densities, these measurements will vary a little bit, but this is okay for making carboy-sized batches here. You'll also need a **measuring ¼ tsp** and **½ tsp** for those additives to be added in tiny amounts. If you don't already have a set of **measuring cups** in your kitchen, get 1- and 2-cup plastic or glass ones for preparing yeast for fermentation and for dissolving additives in water. A cup measures about 237 mL in the US and 250 mL in Canada, but it doesn't matter which you use here.

In addition to the above, you should get a **titration acid test kit** and a **pH meter** for measuring acidity and pH. We'll discuss these and their importance, and choosing a suitable type of pH meter in Chapter FIVE.

When buying equipment, tools, and anything that will come into contact with your wine, be sure that the material is food safe and that it is compatible with wine. Food safe does not guarantee that a material is compatible with wine. Wine has relatively high acidity that can cause substances to leach out of the material into the wine causing not only undesirable effects, but which can be harmful to your health. Glass, food-grade plastics, and stainless steel are all safe. Avoid anything made of brass, copper and iron.

IF MAKING WINE FROM GRAPES

If you want to make a standard 5-gallon (19-liter) batch of wine from grapes, for which you may need up to 100 lbs (45 kg) of fruit (see sidebar on HOW MANY POUNDS OF GRAPES DO I NEED? on p. 49), consider buying the following (Figure 2.8):

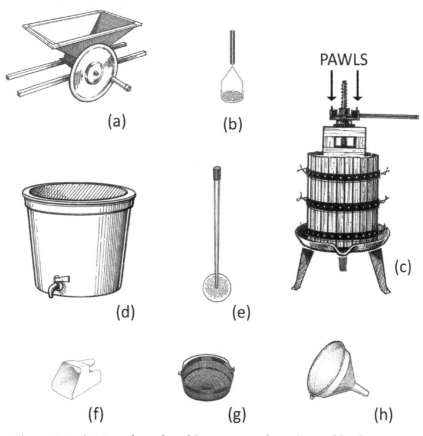

Figure 2.8: a) Manual crusher; b) potato masher; c) wood basket press; d) large food-grade plastic vat; e) punchdown tool; f) plastic scoop; g) plastic colander; h) large funnel

- A basic, inexpensive **manual crusher** for crushing grapes, or, if you don't want to invest in a crusher, you can use, for example, a **potato masher**. A crusher is not to mash grapes, but rather, to split berries open slightly to expose juice to yeast to enable fermentation in red winemaking, or to ease pressing in white winemaking.

- A **wood basket press** for pressing grapes. A no. 30 press can handle the 100 lbs (45 kg) or so of crushed grapes needed to make a carboy of wine. However, a no. 35 press will give you a bit more room to work with, especially if you intend to press whole clusters, i.e., without first crushing grapes. See sidebar on HOW TO USE A BASKET PRESS on p. 51.

  A small **stainless steel press** works well too if you have the patience to do several pressings. You can also use it for making small batches of fruit wines. If you expect to only make very small batches or make wine from kits that include grape skins, a mesh bag that you squeeze by hand will work just fine.

  Presses are not cheap, and you'll likely want to grow your hobby, so make sure to consider your future winemaking needs and purchase a suitably sized press.

- A large **food-grade plastic vat**, something around 13 gal (50 L), as primary fermentor, that can handle 100 lbs (45 kg) of crushed grapes. Your local home winemaking supply shop usually carries these vats or some type of large plastic fermentors; otherwise, you can find them at big-box stores, just make sure that they are food grade.

- A **punchdown tool** for submerging grapes into the fermenting wine; that same potato masher as above will work just fine here too.

- A large **plastic scoop** for transferring grapes at the end of fermentation from the primary fermentor to the press.

- A plastic or stainless steel **colander** or **sieve** to keep grape solids away from wine during the pressing operation.

- A **large funnel** for transferring free- and press-run wine into a carboy.

You can forego the press and primary fermentor and opt instead for a WineEasy (Figure 2.9) for making red wine. The WineEasy is an integrated stainless steel fermentor and press that makes use of a "piston-like" lid that presses the pomace under the action of a vacuum pump, and delivers the pressed wine into a carboy under vacuum.

Figure 2.9: Complete WineEasy system for making red wine

HOW MANY POUNDS OF GRAPES DO I NEED?

For planning purpose to make a standard 5-gal (19-L) batch of white or rosé wine, you'll need around 90 lbs (40 kg) of grapes and about 80 lbs (35 kg) for red wine. These estimates can vary greatly among different varieties as well as from year to year. To avoid not having sufficient wine to fill a carboy, plan on more grapes, say 100 lbs (45 kg), or three 36-lb cases or six 18-lb lugs.

These estimates will give you roughly 6 gal (23 L) of juice or wine, but you'll have more if you buy standard 36-lb cases or 18-lb lugs. You'll need to start with more than 5 gal (19 L) of juice to get to that final volume (about 25 bottles) of wine out of a batch. Pressed juice volume depends on grape variety, grape quality, the type of press you use and how strong you press, as well as how carefully you rack. Some grape varieties produce smaller berries and therefore less juice. A rainy year produces bigger berries with more water, while a hot, dry year produces smaller berries with less juice.

Maceration and fermentation in red winemaking release more juice from grape skins, hence the greater yield compared to whites and rosés, which go straight to the press, crushed or uncrushed, before any fermentation, and therefore release less juice.

It's always best to have more wine to completely fill a carboy than to be short, but be prepared to manage the extra wine in smaller containers, which you'll need to keep full too to avoid spoilage, just like a carboy.

AS YOUR HOBBY GROWS

To simplify or speed up certain tasks, or if you expect to grow your output significantly, you'll want to consider purchasing, or perhaps renting, if available, the following equipment from your local store:

• Manual or electric **crusher–destemmer** (Figure 2.10) to remove stems as you crush grapes.

• A diaphragm- or vacuum-type **pump** (Figure 2.11) for transferring wine between fermentors or for filtering.

• Upgrade to a ½-**inch racking cane** and **hose**, especially if using a pump, for faster processing.

• **Filtration equipment** and **filter pads** or **cartridges**; these are discussed in more detail in Chapter TWELVE.

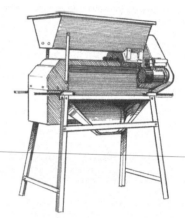

Figure 2.10: Crusher–destemmer

• A good **bottle filler** and **floor corker** to speed up your bottling work; these are discussed in more detail in Chapter THIRTEEN.

The following additional equipment too will come in handy.

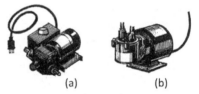

(a)   (b)

Figure 2.11: a) Diaphragm pump; b) vacuum pump

• Measuring teaspoons, tablespoons and cups are okay, but you'll eventually want a good **balance** (gram scale) (Figure 2.12a) that can measure to an accuracy of 1 g, preferably to 0.1 g, for weighing out additives more accurately.

• An **infusion tube** (Figure 2.12b) for easily adding and removing oak chips or cubes when wanting to infuse oak into wine. If you'll be adding oak chips in an open primary fermentor, for example, a pail, you can simply place the chips in a **paint strainer bag**, tie it up with a fishing line or cotton kitchen twine, and simply drop into the juice or fermenting wine.

- A **heating belt** (Figure 2.12c) for keeping wine warm during fermentation if making wine in a colder room.

- An assortment of smaller carboys and jugs, for example, **3-gallon carboys** and **one-gallon jugs,** to manage small volumes in excess of your 5- and 6-gallon carboys.

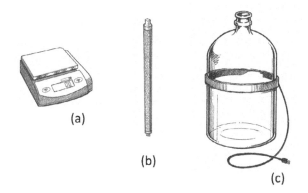

(a)

(b)

(c)

Figure 2.12: a) Balance; b) infusion tube for oak chips; and c) heating belt

HOW TO USE A BASKET PRESS

A basket press is used to extract juice from crushed or uncrushed grapes when making white and rosés wines, or wine from fermented grape solids at the end of fermentation when making reds.

When would one want to press uncrushed grapes? With some grape varieties or styles of wines there is no maceration (soaking) of grape solids in juice. For example, to avoid extracting undesirable substances, such as tannins, when making a fruity-style white wine, or when making a rosé wine from richly colored varieties where maceration would otherwise extract too much color.

To press uncrushed grapes, place a pail under the spout of the press to collect the juice. You'll either need a short pail or container that fits under the spout, or you'll have to raise the press using bricks or cement blocks under the legs of the press. Since you'll want as few grape fragments as possible getting into the juice, place a colander or sieve under the spout. *continued on next page*

Load the press, install the pressing blocks and pressure mechanism making sure that the pawls (see Figure 2.8c) are inserted correctly, that is, the mechanism moves down when you press, then start gradually pressing. Never rush the pressing operation as you'll reduce efficiency and could even damage the press. Instead, press until you feel a strong resistance and there is good flow of juice (or wine). If juice splashes out the sides of the press, you're going too fast. You can otherwise stretch some plastic wrap around the basket to avoid making a mess. As the flow of juice slows down, indicating that some pressure is relieved, then you can press some more. Continue until you've extracted as much juice as desired or possible. While pressing, transfer juice as quickly as possible from the pail to a carboy using a large funnel, and place an airlock and bung on the carboy to protect the juice from the elements. If working with wine that is still fermenting or just completed, don't fill the carboy just yet as gas produced during fermentation will cause foaming and wine to spew out of the carboy. You can either stir the wine for a couple of minutes to remove some gas, or add more wine to the carboy the next day when the wine would have had a chance to "settle down."

When done, reverse the pawls and crank to work the pressure mechanism back up, disassemble the press and break up the pressed grape solids (called the cake) using a pitchfork or a pointed gardening shovel, and discard to the compost or spread throughout your backyard vineyard.

If you're making white or rosé wine and you want a short maceration to extract more of the grape skin substances, such as tannins, aromas, flavors, or color, first crush grapes into a large plastic vat, then use a scoop to transfer the crushed grapes to the press. Have a pail already under the spout as juice will flow from the press right away. Then proceed with pressing as described above; you can expect a much faster extraction of substances, especially color, so be prepared. You'll find more guidelines in Chapter FIFTEEN on how long to macerate to extract the desired color when making rosé wine.

When making red wine, simply transfer the grape solids from the large vat to the press, and press as described above. You'll find more guidelines in Chapter SIXTEEN on the timing of transferring grapes to the press.

CHAPTER THREE

Cleaning and Sanitizing Equipment

R epeated cleaning and sanitizing can seem like daunting tasks, but these are absolutely necessary and must be performed diligently and rigorously. Inadequately cleaned or sanitized equipment can affect quality or cause outright spoilage of juice or wine. Everything—carboys, racking cane, stirring spoon, hoses, pump, anything that will come into contact with juice or wine—must be thoroughly cleaned and properly sanitized to avoid contamination and possible spoilage. These are two separate, non-interchangeable steps—both are needed.

CLEANING

Cleaning involves removing contaminants or residues, like grape fragments, dried juice, soil and dust from the surface of equipment and from every nook and cranny in preparation for sanitizing. This is done by applying mechanical or physical force, such as water pressure or using a scrubbing device, and a suitable cleaning agent and lukewarm water, possibly hot water to deal with stubborn residues.

The most common cleaning agents for winemaking applications, and particularly for removing stubborn red wine stains, are sodium carbonate and sodium percarbonate (the stuff found in many household cleaners and laundry detergents), or commercial products that contain either and which you'll find at your local home winemaking supply store, such as:

- PBW (Powdered Brewery Wash)

- One Step No-Rinse Cleanser (known as Aseptox in Canada)

- B-Brite Cleanser

Always follow manufacturers' instructions and their recommended dilution rates for these products.

To use sodium carbonate or sodium percarbonate, first dissolve in lukewarm water as these don't dissolve well in cooler water. Make up a small amount of solution needed using sodium carbonate at a rate of 3 tbsp per gallon (or about 1 tbsp per liter) of water, or sodium percarbonate at a rate of 1–3 tsp per gallon (or about ¼ to 1 tsp per liter) of water.

Before cleaning equipment, thoroughly rinse with water, pressurized water preferably, then proceed with cleaning. Disperse either solution on the equipment to be cleaned and leave in contact with the surface for 10–20 minutes, then thoroughly rinse with plenty of water followed by a sulfite–citric rinse (see the section SANITIZING) to neutralize any traces of cleaning agent, and finish with one last water rinse.

If, for example, you need to rack two or more batches of wine, you only need to clean and sanitize the first carboy that you'll first rack into, then simply rinse the just-emptied carboy with water and rack the next wine into it.

 Never use a brush or other cleaning device that has a metal component to clean glass carboys. The slightest contact between metal and glass can cause the carboy to shatter and cause serious injury.

 Only use a soft, non-abrasive standard or foam-type sponge for cleaning plastic pails and vats, PET carboys, and anything made of plastic to avoid scratching the material. A scratched surface becomes a perfect breeding ground for spoilage microorganisms.

After cleaning, save whatever solution you used — don't toss it out. You can reuse cleaning solutions several times until they start losing efficacy. They can usually last 3–6 months.

SANITIZING

Sanitizing, sometimes incorrectly referred to as sterilizing, involves removing microbes down to a sufficiently acceptable level that will not pose any winemaking spoilage risks. This is accomplished using a sanitizing agent suitable for the type of material to be sanitized. It is left in contact with the equipment for a minimum amount of time without the need for mechanical force, although that may be necessary or recommended at times.

Sulfite, either sodium metabisulfite or potassium metabisulfite, is the most common and effective sanitizing agent used in winemaking. It is available in crystalline powder or tablet form, the latter known as Campden tablets.

To make a sulfite–citric sanitizing solution, dissolve 3 tbsp of sulfite powder and 1 tbsp of citric acid per gallon (3.8 L) of cool water. Work in a well-ventilated area being careful not to breathe vapor from this solution as it is very strong. Store the solution in an airtight glass or chemical-resistant plastic container; it will last up to 6 months.

To sanitize (following proper cleaning), spray or soak equipment and allow contact for a minimum of 10 minutes, then, optionally, rinse thoroughly with fresh, clean water. If you decide not to rinse or if you do not have fresh water suitable for rinsing, be sure to let the equipment drain well; the tiny amount of residual sulfite after draining is okay.

Do not allow sulfite–citric solution to stay in contact for an extended period of time (e.g., overnight) with certain materials; it can cause pitting on stainless steel material, cracking in silicone bungs, and hoses to become translucent and lose much of their flexibility and suppleness.

Acid-based products too, such as Star San, Saniclean and San Step, are very effective sanitizing agents. Because of their formulations, they are recommended as one-step cleaners/sanitizers, but it is always recommended to clean and sanitize in separate steps. Just a note on the use of Star San: it does cause some foaming, possibly a lot of foaming if agitated vigorously, which can be easily dealt with a water rinse, but it's best not to use with pumps as the foaming can be difficult to remove.

There are also chlorine-based sanitizing agents, which are very effective too, but these can be a source of TCA contamination; TCA is short for 2,4,6-trichloroanisole, the compound responsible for the moldy, musty smell in so-called "corked" wines. Chlorinated powder dust can easily become airborne, find its way into the winemaking area and contaminate equipment, which could then spread out of control throughout the whole area. It can be very difficult, if not impossible, to eradicate a TCA infection. If you want to use bleach, prepare and use solutions outdoors well away from any winemaking equipment or area.

Always follow manufacturers' instructions and observe expiration dates for any of the above products to ensure safety and efficacy.

After you're done using equipment, clean it all up thoroughly, rinse well with fresh water, let dry, and store away in a clean area. There is no need to sanitize equipment for storage purposes; you only need to (clean and) sanitize immediately before use.

As with cleaning solutions, save whatever sanitizing solution you used. You can reuse sanitizing solutions several times until they start losing efficacy. They can usually last 3–6 months.

STORING EMPTY CARBOYS

You can clean carboys and store empty to dry, and then clean again and sanitize when ready to use.

Alternatively, pour ⅛ gallon (500 mL) of sulfite–citric solution into the clean carboy and place a solid bung wrapped in food-grade plastic wrap. The plastic wrap protects the bung from discoloration and damage during long exposures to sulfur dioxide gas from the solution. When ready to use, simply rinse the carboy thoroughly and let drip dry. Save the sulfite–citric solution for storing the next carboy. If storing longer than three months, dump the solution out and add some fresh solution. Easy!

For PET plastic carboys, it's best to store empty and clean and sanitize on the next use.

CHAPTER FOUR

Additives, Additives, Additives! Why So Many Additives?

There are many, many additives and processing aids which can be used in modern winemaking to improve efficiency or speed up certain tasks, deal with specific problems, and improve wine quality. (Refer to the GLOSSARY or the section CAN I MAKE NATURAL WINES—WITHOUT ANY ADDITIVES OR PRESERVATIVES? in Chapter ONE for definitions of the terms "additives" and "processing aids" and why the distinction.)

This chapter lists the most common additives and processing aids, categorized by their main winemaking use, which you'll find at your local home winemaking supply store. Short descriptions will help familiarize yourself with their intended application, so that you can decide if these are appropriate for your use, for example, if you're vegan and wanting to avoid animal-derived additives; you'll find more details on these additives in relevant chapters.

Be sure to read product instructions and additional information in this guide on how to introduce these additives into wine; some may need to be dissolved in water or rehydrated before use to allow swelling, while other additives that dissolve well can be stirred directly into wine. We'll keep it very simple in this guide; all recommended amounts to be added are given in teaspoon (tsp), tablespoon (tbsp) and cup measurements for treating a standard-size carboy.

As for water, if your municipal water is good, good enough to drink unfiltered, and not hard, i.e., it does not have a high mineral content, then it's good to go into your wine; otherwise, buy bottled water—it does not have to be distilled or demineralized water.

In terms of shelf life, except for yeast, bacteria and potassium sorbate, all dry-format additives listed here are good for at least a year when properly stored in a dry, cool area, but only buy what you'll need for any immediate use or for the upcoming winemaking season.

ACIDITY ADJUSTMENTS

Acids. Tartaric, malic, lactic and citric acids are used to increase acidity or decrease pH in low-acidity or high-pH juice or wine. Tartaric acid is usually preferred as it is the most abundant, naturally occurring acid in grapes. You'll also find acid blends made of tartaric, malic and citric acids. These acids and blends all come in crystalline form, except for lactic acid, which usually comes in an 80%–88% solution.

Calcium carbonate. This is known as a *deacidification salt* and comes in powder form. Like potassium bicarbonate and potassium carbonate (see below), it is used to reduce acidity or raise pH in high-acidity or low-pH juice or wine.

Potassium bicarbonate and **potassium carbonate.** Like calcium carbonate, these are deacidification salts used to reduce acidity or raise pH in high-acidity or low-pH juice or wine, and come in powder form.

ALCOHOLIC FERMENTATION

Diammonium phosphate. Also known as DAP. This is a yeast nutrient consisting of inorganic nitrogen, compared to organic nitrogen (from amino acids) in complex yeast nutrients.

Yeast. Also referred to as *cultured yeast* or *active dry yeast.* Yeast is used to conduct the alcoholic fermentation when not wanting to rely on indigenous yeast. It is available in 5-g packets and liquid formats sufficient to make a carboy-sized batch of wine.

There is a limited selection of yeast for making carboy-sized batches; however, some vendors offer a greater selection by repackaging many other yeasts (used by commercial wineries) into small quantities.

Refer to the section CHOOSING WINE YEAST in Chapter SIX for storage guidelines.

Yeast hulls. Yeast hulls are made from dead yeast cells and are used to "detoxify" wine by removing toxic yeast substances that might be causing fermentation problems, for example, a stuck fermentation.

Yeast nutrients. Often referred to as *complex nutrients* as these also contain vitamins, minerals and other substances in addition to organic nitrogen from amino acids. These nutrients are used to feed yeast in conducting a healthy, trouble-free alcoholic fermentation. There are also specific nutrients, called *rehydration nutrients*, used for rehydrating yeast cultures in preparation for fermentation; however, these cannot be used during fermentation. All nutrients come in powder form.

MALOLACTIC FERMENTATION (MLF)

Lysozyme. See *Lysozyme* in the section ENZYMES below.

Malolactic bacteria. Malolactic bacteria are used to conduct MLF (the conversion of malic acid into lactic acid) when not wanting to rely on indigenous bacteria. 2.5-g is the smallest packet size of dry bacterium culture you'll find; it can be used for up to 66 gal (250 L) of wine. These packets can be expensive, so plan carefully and split a packet across different wines. A 2.5-g packet is good for a dozen 5-gal (19-L) carboys and preferably added at the same time to all carboys, or with a very short delay. Alternatively, you can use a liquid format culture better suited for smaller volumes, such as those from White Labs and Wyeast Laboratories.

Refer to the section CONDUCTING MALOLACTIC FERMENTATION in Chapter SEVEN for storage guidelines.

Malolactic nutrients. Often referred to as *complex nutrients* because they also contain vitamins, minerals and other substances in addition to organic nitrogen from amino acids. These nutrients are used to feed bacteria in conducting a healthy, trouble-free MLF. There are also specific nutrients, called *rehydration nutrients*, used for rehydrating bacteria cultures in preparation for MLF. All nutrients come in powder form.

ENZYMES

Lysozyme. An enzyme isolated from egg white used to inhibit malolactic bacteria in wines that have undergone an incomplete MLF or to prevent MLF entirely.

Pectic enzymes. Also called pectolytic enzymes or pectinases. These enzymes break down pectin (a type of starch found in plants) extracted from grape skins and improve settling, clarification, and filterability of wines, as well as improve color and tannin extraction. These enzymes are more important in fruit winemaking where pectin often causes wine to be cloudy. These also ease pressing, improve juice and wine flow through the grape solids in the press, and increase press yield. They are available in powder or liquid forms.

CLARIFICATION (FINING) AND STABILIZATION

Ascorbic acid. Also known as vitamin C. It has high antioxidant power, and as such, it is used when bottling white or rosé wines to scavenge oxygen if the wine will be exposed to air. It is not recommended in reds (see the section OXIDATION in Chapter NINE).

Bentonite. Bentonite is a type of clay with an extraordinary ability to swell in water. It is used to clarify white and rosé wines as well as to remove proteins that could otherwise cause wine to become cloudy.

Campden tablets. See *Sulfite* below.

Carbon. Also known as activated carbon and charcoal. It is used as a last resort to treat serious color and odor faults. It is a very aggressive, nonselective type of fining agent that can remove desirable aromas and flavors. Look for alternative solutions in this guide.

Casein. Casein is a type of protein found in milk, which is highly effective for improving color in white wines affected by oxidation and for reducing tannins in reds.

Chitosan. Chitosan is a type of polysaccharide most often used with silica gel (see *Kieselsol* below) for clarifying white wines. It is also used as a preventative against spoilage yeasts and bacteria (see the section MICROBIAL CONTROL below).

Gelatin. Gelatin powder or liquid is used as a fining agent for taming aggressive tannins in red wines and to compact sediment when using bentonite. It is often used with *Kieselsol* (see below) to avoid over-fining. Winemaking gelatin is derived from connective tissues and skins of pigs.

Isinglass. Isinglass is a protein-type of clarifying agent most effective in white and rosé wines, particularly oak-aged whites, where it enhances aromas without affecting tannins. Though mainly available in powder form as it is more stable, you'll also find it in (liquid) solution form. Isinglass is extracted from the swim bladders of certain fish species.

Kieselsol. Kieselsol is silicon dioxide, i.e., sand, which has been transformed into silica gel, usually as a 30% aqueous solution. It is often used in conjunction with chitosan for clarifying all types of wines as well as for removing proteins and tannins in whites and rosés. It is also used with gelatin to prevent overfining.

Metatartaric acid: A powdered substance used to inhibit the formation of tartrates in young wines meant to be drunk soon after bottling, as an alternative to cold-crashing.

Potassium sorbate. Often simply called sorbate, this is a wine preservative used specifically in preventing renewed fermentation in wines with residual sugar. Only buy as much as you need as it can develop off aromas and flavors with time during storage.

PVPP. Short for polyvinylpolypyrrolidone, PVPP is a synthetic polymer (a very large molecule) with great affinity for polyphenols; it is used to treat browning problems and bitter tannins.

Sparkolloid. Sparkolloid is a proprietary powdered fining agent derived from brown algae. It is particularly effective in settling finely suspended particles and is therefore recommended for red wines but also suitable for whites and rosés.

Sulfite. This is the generic name for the various sulfur-based substances used as wine preservatives against oxidation and microbial spoilage. These are available in powder or tablet forms. The most common are potassium metabisulfite and sodium metabisulfite. Potassium metabisulfite is preferred over sodium metabisulfite to minimize the amount of sodium added to wine, however small that amount may be. The powdered form can be simply dissolved in a little water while so-called Campden tablets must first be crushed to a powder.

MICROBIAL CONTROL

Chitosan. In addition to being an excellent clarifying agent, chitosan can be used as a preventive against spoilage yeasts and bacteria.

Lysozyme. See *Lysozyme* in the section ENZYMES.

Sulfite. See *Sulfite* in the section CLARIFICATION (FINING) AND STABILIZATION.

COLOR STABILITY, MOUTHFEEL, AND OAK

Gum arabic: An additive made from natural gum extracted from acacia trees, primarily used in wine to increase mouthfeel, to give a sense of "fullness" in the mouth. It is available in powder form or as a 20%–30% liquid solution.

Inactivated yeast. Also referred to as inactive dry yeast (IDY) and specific inactivated yeast (SIY), it refers to a range of yeast-derived products used for stabilizing color in reds, enhancing structure, and "rounding" tannins for improved mouthfeel. These products can be hard to find as they are packaged in large formats for commercial wineries, but some retailers repackage select products for small-scale winemaking.

Oak. Oak has great affinity with wine, especially red wines. You can add oak powder, chips, segments, spirals, even (liquid) oak extract—whatever your local store carries—to add a layer of oak aromas and flavors to your wine. Oak wood is loaded with beneficial tannins that can improve mouthfeel, body, and color. Oak products also come from various countries and in different toast levels, i.e., light, medium, medium-plus, and heavy. Each can impart different aromas and flavors to your wine.

Tannins. Tannin additives are sourced from grape skins and certain types of wood, though primarily white oak wood. These are used to enhance mouthfeel, complexity, body, and stabilize color in red wines. These improve aging (tannins are natural antioxidants), and can also reduce the vegetal, green pepper-like character in some red wines, particularly those made from underripe Cabernet varieties as well as Malbec. Tannins are available in deep-brown-colored powder or liquid forms.

SUGAR AND SWEETENERS

Glycerin. Glycerin is a liquid additive used to improve mouthfeel and to add sweetness without the worry of refermentation. Glycerin cannot be metabolized by yeast.

Sugar. You'll often need to add sugar to juice in order to increase the amount of alcohol to be produced, a technique known as *chaptalization*. You may also want to increase sweetness, perhaps to balance high acidity. Table sugar (sucrose) is the most readily available product and works well for either purpose. You can also use glucose or fructose. For sweetening wine, you can also use a wine conditioner or other kinds of natural or artificial sweeteners, such as honey and stevia.

Wine conditioner. A liquid solution made of sugar and sorbate for sweetening wine.

CHAPTER FIVE

Basic Wine Analysis and Adjustments

*Y*ou can make great wines, consistently, with only a basic knowledge of wine chemistry and minimal wine analysis. You can avoid problems by doing some simple, routine checks of fermentation progress and acidity. It's always easier to monitor wine and make adjustments, when needed, as opposed to running into problems and dealing with flawed or even spoiled wine.

This chapter deals with the three most important aspects of managing quality in your winemaking: specific gravity, acidity and sulfur dioxide. It describes how to measure sugar levels in juice, how to make adjustments to get to a desired alcohol level, how to monitor fermentation progress and confirm completion, and how to evaluate and adjust acidity and pH for better-balanced wine.

Sulfur dioxide (SO_2) is a more advanced topic and requires equally advanced techniques and equipment, but this guide provides practical advice to help you manage sulfites without the burden of getting into the technical analysis. Once you become more comfortable with this topic and you're ready to tackle the science of it all, you can read about SO_2 chemistry in *Modern Home Winemaking*.

This chapter is the most challenging, and you'll likely have to return to it occasionally. That's okay as concepts will become clearer once you start making wine and measuring the various parameters.

SPECIFIC GRAVITY AND POTENTIAL ALCOHOL

Making wine is about the conversion of sugars into alcohol, more specifically, glucose and fructose into ethanol, and the amount of sugars present in juice can be estimated by measuring Specific Gravity, which is used to determine the amount of alcohol that can be produced.

Specific Gravity (SG) is a measure of juice or wine density relative to the density of water, which is 1.000, both measured at 68°F (20°C). This measurement provides a very good approximation of the amount of sugars in juice, which winemakers often refer to as OG for original gravity.

SG is unitless and should always be reported using three decimal digits, for example, 1.092, not 1.09. The decimal digits are called *points*, so that when the SG drops, for example, from 1.092 to 1.080, it is said to have dropped 12 points. SG of grape juice will be between 1.080 and 1.110 for making wine in normal alcohol range.

Many winemakers use the °Brix scale (the degree sign is often omitted for simplicity), which expresses the amount of sugars as a mass (weight) percentage measured at 68°F (20°C); for example, 22.0 Brix means that the juice contains 22.0% sugar by weight, or 22.0 g of sugars in 100 g of juice. This guide uses SG since it is most commonly used by home winemakers.

Measuring Specific Gravity and Potential Alcohol

Potential Alcohol (PA) refers to the maximum amount of alcohol that can be produced if all sugars are fermented and SG falls to less than 1.000. The actual amount of alcohol produced depends on the amount of sugars that was fermented, which can be determined by measuring the final SG and PA at the end of fermentation.

PA and actual alcohol produced are expressed as % alcohol/volume, or % alc/vol, as you see on any bottle of wine, and most wines are in the range 11%–15% alc/vol. Winemakers most often talk in terms of % ABV or simply ABV, which stands for Alcohol By Volume and means the same as % alcohol/volume.

This guide uses PA to refer to potential alcohol as measured in juice, before fermentation, and % ABV to refer to the final amount of alcohol in wine at the end of fermentation.

Table 5.1 lists SG and PA ranges to produce various styles of wines.

Table 5.1: SG and PA ranges for different styles of wines. Numbers have been rounded for simplicity. Refer to your hydrometer for more accurate values and conversions.

Style of wine	SG	PA (% alc/vol)
Dry, light, fruity white or rosé	1.080–1.090	11–12.5
Off-dry, light, fruity white or rosé	1.080–1.090	11–12.5
Medium-sweet, fruity white or rosé	1.080–1.090	11–12.5
Sweet, fruity white or rosé	1.080–1.090	11–12.5
Fuller-bodied or oak-aged white	1.090–1.100	12.5–13.5
Light- to medium-bodied red	1.090–1.100	12.5–13.5
Full-bodied red	1.100–1.110	13.5–15

A wine is said to be fermented "dry" when there are no more sugars to ferment and the final SG is 0.995 or lower. If fermentation stops on its own or is purposely halted when the SG is greater than 1.000, less alcohol would have been produced than the measured PA, and there will be some residual unfermented sugars that will affect taste as well as wine stability. Yeast can start fermenting residual sugars if conditions become ideal, and if it happens in bottles, corks can pop out or, in the worst case, bottles can explode.

The amount of unfermented sugars remaining in wine is referred to as residual sugars (RS); it also includes any sugar added as a sweetener. RS is expressed in grams per liter (g/L) or simply as a percentage of sugar mass to wine volume; for example, 2 g/L and 0.2% RS are the same. Sweetening is discussed in Chapter TEN. Measuring RS is an advanced topic and requires more advanced analytical tools and techniques.

You'll find many tables in the literature and online converting between SG and PA, and which often don't concord; that's because different yeasts convert sugars into alcohol differently under varying conditions, and some alcohol is blown off during fermentation—it's far from an exact science—and therefore winemakers use different factors. We'll keep it simple here and rely on the trusted triple-scale hydrometer (Figure 5.1), the instrument used to measure SG, Brix and PA; this is the type included with starter kits and the most commonly used in home winemaking. You can also refer to Table 5.2 below when you need to convert between SG and PA; it uses a conversion factor used on most home winemaking hydrometers.

Figure 5.1: Triple-scale hydrometer

Inexpensive hydrometers can measure up to SG 1.150 and 20% PA, and with such large ranges, you cannot expect to make very accurate measurements (hence the use of approximate numbers in examples), but it's all good for our purpose here.

Basic triple-scale home winemaking hydrometers are calibrated at 60°F (15.5°C), which means you should adjust readings up or down if measuring SG at temperatures other than the calibration temperature and if outside the range 50°F–68°F (10°C–20°C). But in most cases you'll find the adjustments to be only minor and unnecessary given the inherent error of the hydrometer in such complex liquids as juice and wine. If you want to make adjustments:

- Subtract 0.001 if temperature is below 50°F (10°C)
- Add 0.001 if temperature is in the range 68°F–77°F (20°C–25°C)
- Add 0.002 if temperature is above 77°F (25°C)

Measure SG, PA and temperature of juice before fermentation starts, then during fermentation to monitor progress, and when fermentation is complete so that you can make a final determination of % ABV based on the initial PA.

To take a reading with a hydrometer, sanitize the hydrometer and cylinder, insert the hydrometer into the cylinder, then, using a sanitized wine thief or gravy baster, draw a small amount of juice or wine from the fermentor and transfer to the cylinder right to the top, let the hydrometer

Table 5.2: Approximate conversions between SG and PA commonly used on most home winemaking hydrometers.

SG	PA	SG	PA	SG	PA
0.990	0.0	1.038	5.1	1.080	10.7
0.995	0.0	1.040	5.3	1.082	10.9
1.000	0.0	1.042	5.6	1.084	11.2
1.002	0.3	1.044	5.9	1.086	11.5
1.004	0.5	1.046	6.1	1.088	11.7
1.006	0.8	1.048	6.4	1.090	12.0
1.008	1.1	1.050	6.7	1.092	12.3
1.010	1.3	1.052	6.9	1.094	12.5
1.012	1.6	1.054	7.2	1.096	12.8
1.014	1.9	1.056	7.5	1.098	13.1
1.016	2.1	1.058	7.7	1.100	13.3
1.018	2.4	1.060	8.0	1.102	13.6
1.020	2.7	1.062	8.3	1.104	13.9
1.022	2.9	1.064	8.5	1.106	14.1
1.024	3.2	1.066	8.8	1.108	14.4
1.026	3.5	1.068	9.1	1.110	14.7
1.028	3.7	1.070	9.3	1.112	14.9
1.030	4.0	1.072	9.6	1.114	15.2
1.032	4.3	1.074	9.9	1.116	15.5
1.034	4.5	1.076	10.1	1.118	15.7
1.036	4.8	1.078	10.4	1.120	16.0

float and stabilize, and take readings on the SG and PA scales at the meniscus level (Figure 5.2). Note that each line on the SG scale on the hydrometer represents 2 points, and each on the PA scale represents 1% alcohol. Make sure the hydrometer floats freely without touching the base or sides of the cylinder; if it does, the cylinder is too small or you need to pour more juice or wine.

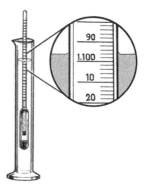

Figure 5.2: How to take a hydrometer reading. SG here is 1.096, i.e., three lines below 1.090

When making red wine where grape skins macerate in the juice, the grape solids will make it difficult to draw juice. Thoroughly mix the juice and grape solids, immerse a sanitized strainer or sieve deep enough into the grape solids to separate solids from the juice, and then use a sanitized wine thief or gravy baster to draw a sample—it's very easy.

Although you can simply drop a sanitized hydrometer in the juice to take a reading, it is safest to draw a sample and transfer it to a test cylinder. This way, if your hydrometer breaks, it will not contaminate—or possibly spoil—the whole batch. You also can't take a valid reading by dropping in a hydrometer when fermenting with grape skins.

Measure SG once daily during fermentation to monitor progress, to make sure all is proceeding okay. At this stage, wine contains a lot of carbon dioxide (CO_2) gas from fermentation, which will make your hydrometer readings look higher than actual. To get more accurate readings, stir the sample with the hydrometer right in the test cylinder and give it a good spin (Figure 5.3) to remove as much gas as possible.

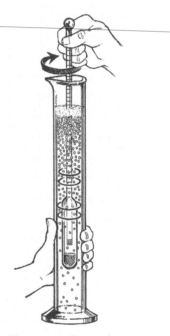

Fermentation is complete and the final % ABV will be close to the measured PA when SG reads 0.995 or lower and has been stable for two consecutive days. However, if the wine has stopped fermenting or you deliberately stopped fermentation for a sweeter style of wine, then you have to subtract the final PA from the initial PA. More importantly, you'll need to stabilize any wine that contains residual sugar, that is, any wine that has not fermented to SG 0.995 or lower. Wine stabilization is described further in Chapter NINE.

Figure 5.3: Degassing a fermenting wine sample

You cannot reliably measure the amount of residual sugar at the end of fermentation using a hydrometer. There are many online calculators that convert SG readings into RS, but there can be significant differences. What's important here is that any wine with a final SG above 0.995 contains sufficient sugars to restart fermentation at some point in time, perhaps in bottles.

Let's look at a couple of examples to understand how this all works in practical terms.

EXAMPLE

Determining SG, PA, and % ABV in a wine fermented to dryness

You just received your load of white grapes, crushed and pressed, and took a sample of cold juice. You measured SG 1.094 and about 12.5% PA at 50°F (10°C) using your triple-scale hydrometer calibrated at 60°F (15.5°C). Given the difference in temperature, you can correct the SG by subtracting 0.001 so that the adjusted SG is 1.093, still about 12.5%.

You ferment the wine to final SG 0.994, and therefore, the ABV should be about 12.5%. Since SG is below 0.995, the wine can be safely considered stable and not require any stabilization treatment.

EXAMPLE

Determining SG, PA, and % ABV in a wine not fermented to dryness

From the example above, you measured SG 1.093 and about 12.5% PA, but now, fermentation stopped at SG 1.008, or about 1% PA.

The final ABV is calculated as 12.5 − 1.0, or 11.5%.

Now, let's say you measured SG 1.076 and 10% PA initially, but you want to make a white wine with 12.5% ABV, or, on the flip side, you measured SG 1.120 and a whopping 16% PA, which would be too strong and, aside from possible fermentation problems at that high alcohol, you prefer this red wine to have around 13.5% ABV. How do you make adjustments to get the juice to the desired SG and PA targets? The answers: chaptalization and amelioration, respectively.

Chaptalization

Chaptalization is the practice of adding (fermentable) sugar to juice to increase SG and PA, when, for example, a weak, rainy vintage did not produce grapes with sufficient sugars.

You'll need to add approximately 17.5 grams of sugar for every liter of juice to raise PA by about 1%, or to raise SG by about 7 points. That works out to about 66 grams or 2.3 oz per gallon.

Table sugar (sucrose) is most convenient for chaptalizing. You'll need about 2½ cups per pound or ½ cup per 100 g of sugar.

You can also use glucose or fructose (yeast prefers glucose and ferments it to a cleaner finish), or even concentrate, but the calculations get tricky with the latter as you don't know the sugar concentration, therefore, when chaptalizing with concentrate, add in small amounts—which you should do with any additions anyways—and measure SG and PA after every addition, and continue adding more until you hit your desired numbers.

Once you have determined the amount of sugar to add, add only half that amount, re-measure SG and PA, and if these are halfway between your starting and target SG and PA numbers, you can add the other half. If you are over or under your SG and PA with the half addition, you need to adjust your second addition accordingly.

This half-addition approach is particularly useful when chaptalizing juice with crushed grapes, as in red winemaking, since you don't know the exact volume of juice, and so, you have to estimate the volume and make additions and adjustments accordingly.

These calculations can get tricky if math is not your thing; you can download the CALCULATOR FOR CHAPTALIZING JUICE at Modern HomeWinemaking.com to help you figure this all out.

To add sugar to juice, first dissolve the calculated amount of sugar in a small volume of juice preferably; water is okay although it will somewhat dilute the juice or must. You'll need about ¼ gal (1 L) of juice or water per 1 lb (500 g) of sugar. Thoroughly stir the syrupy solution for 5 to 10 minutes or until all the sugar is completely dissolved. No heating is necessary; it is never advisable to heat juice (or wine). Sugar dissolves adequately at room temperature, though it will take longer at cooler temperatures. Once fully dissolved, add to the rest of the batch and stir until well mixed. Note that there will be a small volume increase due to the added sugar (and water, if used). Let rest for about an hour, stir thoroughly again, then take a sample and re-measure SG and PA to confirm you have chaptalized correctly to your target numbers.

It's always best to add sugar to juice, as opposed to during fermentation, because the sudden addition of sugar can shock yeast and cause fermentation problems. You can also expect a messy eruption if you are not careful adding the sugar.

Let's look at an example of chaptalization.

EXAMPLE

Chaptalization using sucrose (table sugar)

You just crushed and pressed some 100 lbs (45 kg) of white grapes into about 6 gal (23 L) of juice, taken a sample, and measured SG 1.084 and about 11% PA, but you want a dry wine with 12.5% ABV—an increase of 1.5% or about 11 or 12 SG points. So you need to chaptalize to around SG 1.096 and 12.5% PA.

Using the conversion factor of 66 g/gal per 1% PA increase, you need to add 66 g/gal × 1.5%, or about 100 g/gal. Then the total amount of sucrose (table sugar) to add for your batch is:

$$\text{Total amount of sugar to add (g)} = 100 \ ^g/_{gal} \times 6 \, \text{gal}$$
$$= 600 \, \text{g (about 3 cups)}$$

Since the juice volume is an estimate, you need to be careful and only add about half the calculated amount of sucrose, 300 g or about 1½ cups, as per instructions described above, re-measure SG and PA, and proceed with the second half-addition if you measured around SG 1.090 and just under 12% PA.

Amelioration

Amelioration is the practice of adding water to juice to bring SG and PA down to a desired target, when, for example, a hot, dry vintage produced excessive amounts of sugars in grapes and which would produce too much alcohol and surely cause fermentation to stop well before dryness.

A significant amount of water may be required to lower SG and PA, and this will cause acids, aromas, flavors, color (in reds) and everything else to become diluted, hence why you should always seek juice or grapes that are not excessively high in SG and PA, unless you are prepared to ameliorate. The secondary issue—and not a trivial one—is that amelioration can significantly increase total volume of your batch beyond the capacity of your fermentor (pail or carboy).

To mitigate dilution, at least with regards to acidity, acidulate (add acid to) the water to be added to the same acidity as measured in juice; use tartaric acid for this purpose. We'll explore acidity in the next section.

As with chaptalization, add half the calculated amount of acidulated water, re-measure SG and PA, and add the other half, making adjustments as required. Use the Pearson Square to calculate the amount of water needed.

The Pearson Square (Figure 5.4) is a simple tool to calculate the *number of parts* of juice (or wine) of a given concentration required to bring the concentration of another volume of juice or wine to a desired level.

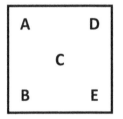

A = the concentration of the wine to be used for the "correction"
B = the concentration of the wine to be corrected
C = the desired concentration
D = the number of parts of wine to be used and is equal to C−B
E = the number of parts of wine to be corrected and is equal to A−C
If D or E results in a negative value, enter the absolute (positive) value.

Figure 5.4: Pearson Square

Let's look at an example of amelioration.

EXAMPLE

Amelioration

You just crushed and pressed some 100 lbs (45 kg) of red grapes into an estimated volume of about 6 gal (23 L) of juice, taken a sample, and measured SG 1.120 and about 16% PA, and total acidity of 6.0 g/L (0.6%), but you want a dry red with approximately 13.5% ABV. Now you need to figure out how much acidulated water you need to add to lower PA from 16% to 13.5%.

Enter the numbers in the Pearson Square, where A is the PA of water, so zero, B is the PA of the juice, i.e., 16.0, C is the desired PA of 13.5, then D is 16.0 – 13.5, or 2.5, and E is 0 – 13.5, or 13.5.

0		2.5
	13.5	
16.0		13.5

The Pearson Square says that you need 2.5 parts of water to 13.5 parts of juice to lower PA from 16% to 13.5%, and therefore, for the estimated 6 gal (23 L) of juice:

$$Volume\ of\ water\ needed\ (gal) = 6\ gal \times \frac{2.5}{13.5} = 1.1\ gal\ (let's\ call\ it\ 1\ gal)$$

Now, add 6.0 g/L of tartaric acid to the one gallon (3.8 liters) of water, not the juice, to match the acidity of the juice, and dissolve well. The amount to add is calculated as follows:

$$Amount\ of\ tartaric\ acid\ to\ add\ (g) = 6.0\ ^g/_L \times 3.8\ L$$
$$= 22.8\ g\ (about\ 1½\ tbsp\ assuming\ about\ 15\ g\ in\ a\ tbsp)$$

Only add half a gallon (about 2 liters) of the acidulated water to the juice and stir well, then re-measure SG and PA, and proceed with the second half-addition if you measured just under 15% PA.

This example illustrates that a significant amount of water, 17% of the juice volume, is required to lower PA by just 2.5% alc/vol.

You can download my AMELIORATION CALCULATOR at <u>Modern HomeWinemaking.com</u> to help you figure this all out more easily.

ACIDITY AND pH

In Chapter ONE it was highlighted the importance of acidity in making balanced wine. Often, juice (if not already adjusted by your producer or purveyor) and grapes will need an adjustment if acidity is low due to, for example, a hot growing season, or, on the flip side, if acidity is high due to, for example, a poor, cold growing season. Or you may be faced with high pH because of lots of potassium, a naturally occurring mineral transported from the soil to the grapes. These cases can be both confusing and a challenge to deal with, so let's take a look at some basic concepts to make sense of it all.

What are acidity and pH?

Total acidity, or TA, is a measurement of the concentration of all acids in juice and wine. In juice, tartaric and malic are the two major acids; there many, many more acids, but they exist in tiny concentrations, and although those too are measured, we won't need to worry about them. In wine too tartaric (see sidebar on TARTARIC ACID AND TARTRATES) and malic are the major acids, but wines that have undergone malolactic fermentation (MLF) contain lactic acid instead of malic acid. Chapter SEVEN discusses malolactic fermentation and the conversion of malic acid into lactic acid, and how this affects acidity and pH.

Yeast fermentation also produces a new acid, succinic acid, which is often not mentioned in acidity discussions, but it's an important one because it can represent a significant percentage of the total acidity.

Acetic acid is another important acid because, when detected by smell, it points to a winemaking problem, although it is always present in small undetectable amounts that actually enhance a wine's aromatic complexity. Acetic acid is the acid of vinegar and that is its characteristic odor. Winemakers refer to acetic acid as volatile acidity, or VA, because it can be smelled, whereas the other acids mentioned above are non-volatile, and so, you cannot smell those although each contributes specific taste nuances.

TARTARIC ACID AND TARTRATES

Tartaric acid is the main acid of interest in winemaking as it is the most abundant in grapes. Unlike malic acid, tartaric acid is not metabolized by yeast or bacteria under normal winemaking conditions; however, it has a special chemical property that can cause an instability that must be managed.

In a nutshell, tartaric acid can react with naturally occurring potassium to form potassium bitartrate, which is the chemical name for cream of tartar. Under cold conditions, for example, when wine is refrigerated for some period of time, potassium bitartrate will crystallize and precipitate as tartrate crystals, or tartrates, also called wine diamonds. Tartrates can be alarming to novices as the crystals look like tiny shards of glass but these are completely harmless. Cream of tartar powder used for baking goods is in fact produced from tartrate crystals. Winemakers put the wine through a cold treatment before bottling to avoid crystals forming in bottles.

Now, since tartaric acid drops as tartrates, there is a commensurate drop in total acidity (TA), and given the inverse relationship between acidity and pH, one could easily jump to the conclusion that pH increases. It's not that simple! But we'll keep it simple here and only state the net effect: when wine pH is below 3.65, both TA and pH decrease, while when wine pH is above 3.65, then, the inverse relationship holds—TA decreases and pH increases. Why is this important?

If you are already having to deal with a case of low TA or a high pH, these acidity and pH changes can further exacerbate these challenging conditions. You therefore have to be mindful of this special behavior of tartaric acid and manage your winemaking accordingly.

Tartrates do form preferentially under cold conditions, however, since potassium bitartrate has poor solubility in alcohol, tartrates also form during fermentation as juice transforms into wine with increasing alcohol. During fermentation, tartrates get buried in the lees, i.e., the spent yeast cells and other sediment that form at the bottom of the carboy. It is not uncommon to see acidity drop due to tartrates during fermentation, although the net change in total acidity depends on what happens with other acids during fermentation.

Measuring Acidity and pH

Since there are a lot of different acids in juice and wine, we have to measure the sum of all acids, known as total acidity, or TA, and often and more correctly referred to as total titratable acidity. To simplify matters, we will assume that all acids are equivalent to tartaric acid so that acidity measurements can be expressed in g/L or as a percentage and as tartaric acid equivalent. For example, 5.0 g/L or 0.50% TA means that the sum of all acids is equivalent to 5.0 g/L if all acids are considered tartaric acid. The percentage notation seems most common among amateurs, but g/L is clearer, so that's the notation we'll use here.

It also gets a touch more confusing. The many acids all have different strengths, but you can't tell how strong from TA measurements. Two wines with the same TA but opposite amounts of tartaric and malic acids will taste very different. So we need to look at how strong each acid is; this is the concept of pH. In simple terms, pH is a measure of the strength of an acid, or all acids in a complex solution like wine.

You'll recall from high school chemistry that there is an inverse relationship between acidity and pH, in that, the higher the acidity, the lower the pH, and vice versa. But pH is also highly influenced by the presence of potassium minerals; a high pH in juice and wine may be due to the presence of great amounts of potassium that can exacerbate tartrate instability (see sidebar on TARTARIC ACID AND TARTRATES).

Why is this all important? Because wine is best enjoyed when it is properly balanced, and acidity is a big part of that equation. Low or high acidity can detract from enjoyment, and high pH makes wine susceptible to shortfalls, such as poorer color (in reds) and shorter aging potential, and prone to microbial spoilage since microbes thrive at higher pH. It's therefore imperative to measure TA and pH throughout the process to make good wine and consistently so year after year.

The target TA depends on your palate and desired style of wine, and the taste of wine is influenced also by alcohol, tannins, and any residual sugars. As we have seen in the section ABOUT ALCOHOL, ACIDITY, SWEETNESS, AND TANNINS in Chapter ONE, sugar reduces the perception of acidity while acidity reinforces the bitterness of tannins, but keep in mind that colder serving temperatures augment the perception of acidity. That's why whites generally have more acidity and are served colder, to give them freshness, whereas reds tend to have lower acidity, especially full-bodied reds with their loads of tannins, and served at warmer temperatures so as not to have acidity and tannins clash. As for pH, juice and wine are usually between 3 and 4.

Table 5.3 lists recommended ranges for TA and pH in juice and for different styles of wines. These are only guidelines to help you make decisions initially, but you'll learn how to assess acidity by taste before jumping into making adjustments based on targets and which may not be necessary. You'll come to develop your own palate and taste; your numbers may become different from these guidelines, likely in a narrower range, and that's okay.

Table 5.3: Recommended TA and pH ranges for juice and different styles of wines (divide TA by 10 to convert from g/L to %)

	JUICE	WINE	
Style of wine	TA range (g/L)	TA range (g/L)	pH range
Dry white or rosé	5–10	5–8	3.1–3.4
Off-dry white or rosé	7–12	6–10	3.1–3.4
Light-bodied red	5–8	5–7	3.3–3.6
Full-bodied red	4–7	4–6	3.3–3.6

TA should be measured at every key checkpoint in your winemaking: in juice, after fermentation, both alcoholic and malolactic, and after cold stabilization. TA is very easily measured by a procedure called titration using an inexpensive acid testing kit (Figure 5.5) that includes: a 10-mL syringe, small beaker, phenolphthalein solution (a color indicator), and sodium hydroxide (NaOH) solution. The NaOH solution should have its concentration clearly printed on the label; it should read something like $0.1N$, $0.133N$ or $0.2N$. You'll need to know this concentration value to calculate TA at the end of titration. You'll also want to get a second 10-mL syringe, or better yet, a 10-mL pipette to measure out exact volumes of juice or wine.

Titration involves adding NaOH, one drop at a time, to a juice or wine sample until the acids are neutralized, at which point, known as the titration endpoint, the color turns pink for white samples or greyish-green for red samples when using phenolphthalein as the indicator that you have reached the titration endpoint. The volume of NaOH dispensed to neutralize all the acids is then used to calculate TA.

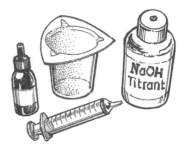

Figure 5.5: Acid titration kit

The color change to pink for white samples is easy to detect although some wonder how deep a pink it should be—it should be a faint and persistent pink. The color change for red samples is more challenging because of the darker color. The sample turns a greyish color while adding NaOH, then a greenish color at the titration endpoint.

To get more accurate, consistent results and to avoid having to deal with color changes, skip the phenolphthalein and use instead a pH meter and titrate until the pH reaches 8.2.

To measure TA using a pH meter, transfer *exactly* 10 mL of juice or *degassed* wine to a 100-mL beaker using a 10-mL pipette, and add *fresh distilled water* to bring the volume to about 50 mL. The amount of distilled water does not need to be precise. Your kit's instructions as to the sample volume and amount of water to add may be different, but the process is identical.

Wine may contain significant amounts of gas leftover from fermentation, and this gas behaves like an acid in wine and will skew your measurements, hence why you must first degas wine samples. Draw a 15-mL sample into a test tube or small glass container with lid, and shake vigorously for a few minutes to release the gas out; open the test tube or container after each shaking to release pressure, and then repeat. The 15-mL sample will be short because of the gas just expelled, but you'll have enough now to draw 10 mL for titration.

Use your 10-mL syringe to draw *exactly* 10 mL of fresh NaOH solution no older than six months. If you see any air bubbles in the syringe, flip it upside-down, tap on it to get the bubble to float to the top, then push on the plunger to expel the air bubble out being careful not to spill NaOH solution. You may need to draw more NaOH to get back to the 10-mL mark.

Insert the electrode of the pH meter into the sample, stir very gently, and wait for the reading to stabilize. During titration, gently stir the sample to get a proper pH reading; either swirl the beaker, stir gently with the electrode, or use a magnetic stirrer—you can buy one fairly inexpensively.

Very carefully add one drop of NaOH solution into the sample using the syringe. You'll notice the pH starting to rise slowly with each drop of NaOH. Continue adding NaOH solution *one drop at a time* until the pH approaches 8.0. Wait for the pH reading to stabilize after each drop. Be careful while approaching 8.2 as pH will shoot up very quickly—it's easy to overshoot. When the pH reading is stable at 8.2, stop—titration is complete. Read the volume of NaOH solution dispensed from the syringe, and follow your kit's instructions to calculate TA.

The calculation provided with kits assumes that you are using NaOH solution with a given concentration, usually $0.1N$, $0.133N$ or $0.2N$. That calculation is based on the following formula that you can use for any NaOH concentration or sample volume:

$$TA\,(g/L) = \frac{75 \times mL\ NaOH \times N\ NaOH}{mL\ of\ sample}$$

Simply divide by 10 the result of the above calculation to express TA as a %; for example, 6.4 g/L can be expressed as 0.64%.

EXAMPLE

Calculating TA from titration

You used 8.5 mL of $0.1N$ NaOH to titrate a 10-mL sample of wine. Calculate TA, expressed in g/L as tartaric acid equivalents, as follows:

$$TA\,(g/L) = \frac{75 \times 8.5 \times 0.1}{10.0} = 6.4\ g/L$$

We just saw how to use a pH meter to monitor pH during titration. You'll also be using a pH meter to monitor pH in each step of your winemaking to make sure that it is within range. Too high a pH points to very low acidity or high potassium, which makes wine highly susceptible to oxidation problems and microbial spoilage. If you're not yet ready to invest in a pH meter, you can start with pH strips; these are okay, but not great because they are not very accurate, especially that they involve assessing a color change—not always easy, and you won't be able to use pH strips for titrations. A pH meter is a smart investment.

Figure 5.6: Inexpensive pen-style pH meter

There are many types and models of pH meters in a wide range of prices. If you're just starting off, get an inexpensive pen-style portable meter with integrated electrode (Figure 5.6) that reads to one decimal digit, e.g., 3.5. As your hobby and technical know-how grow, consider getting a pH meter that measures and reads to two decimal digits, e.g., 3.55, and with automatic temperature compensation for greater accuracy and better control of your wines. Since pH is a logarithmic function, there is a fairly significant difference, for example, between pH 3.50 and 3.60.

The key to getting good, accurate results is regular calibration and proper maintenance of your pH meter. Refer to your pH meter's instructions on how to calibrate, and on the proper use, care, and maintenance.

To measure pH with a pH meter without temperature compensation, first adjust the temperature of the sample to about 77°F (25°C), dip the electrode in the sample and *stir gently* either with the electrode or with a magnetic stirrer. Wait for the reading to stabilize—it should take no more than 30 seconds. When done, rinse the electrode with distilled water and store in a storage solution. If the reading drifts and takes too long to stabilize, the electrode is either out of calibration, dirty or no longer good. Electrodes can last easily two years or more if properly maintained.

Very often, you'll have to deal with juice or grapes that are less than perfect from an unusually hot, cold or rainy growing season, perhaps due to poor vineyard management or an ill-timed harvest, or even because of storage or transportation problems. Acidity (TA) or pH, perhaps both, will be too low or too high, and you need to make adjustments to bring either or both within range to still make a balanced wine.

Let's look at how to make acidity and pH adjustments keeping in mind that these are best done at the juice stage, that is, before fermentation, to allow better integration of acidity with the wine and to avoid fermentation problems. You can still make adjustments after fermentation, but only small adjustments preferably, not more than 1 to 1.5 g/L. Never make adjustments during fermentation, which could adversely affect yeast and fermentation. It's worth repeating:

Make acid adjustments before fermentation, only small changes after fermentation, and never during an active fermentation.

Here, we'll only look at making adjustments in juice that have either low TA and high pH, or the opposite, high TA and low pH, so that an increase in one causes a decrease in the other. Juice with both low TA and pH, or both high TA and pH are very tricky to deal with and require some experience, but these special cases are much less common.

Acidification

When acidity is too low or pH is too high, you can add an acid to increase acidity—this is referred to as acidification.

To raise TA or lower pH, add 1 g/L of tartaric acid for each 1 g/L TA you want to raise. You should be able to hit your target TA quite easily since it's a simple acid addition. However, the corresponding drop in pH is not straightforward because of some underlying complex chemistry (it's called buffering, if you want to research this further), and therefore, if the goal is to adjust pH, it's best to make stepwise acid adjustments until you hit your target. But the drop should be in the order of 0.1 for every 1 g/L of tartaric acid you add. As with all additions, to play it safe, only add half the calculated amount, take a measurement to confirm that the addition matches your calculations, and then do the second half-addition.

Let's look at a couple of examples.

EXAMPLE

Acidification with tartaric acid for the purpose of increasing TA

You just crushed and pressed some 100 lbs (45 kg) of white grapes into about 6 gal (23 L) of juice, then taken a sample and measured 4.0 g/L TA and pH 3.35.

You want to increase TA by 2.0 g/L to 6.0 g/L to make a more refreshing white wine with zippier acidity. Calculate as follows the amount of tartaric acid to add:

$$\text{Total amount of tartaric acid to add (g)} = 2.0\,\text{g/L} \times 23\,\text{L}$$
$$= 46\,\text{g (about 3 tbsp)}$$

Add half that amount to the juice, so 23 g or about 1½ tbsp, mix thoroughly, and take a new sample and re-measure TA and pH. Your TA should now be around 5.0 g/L, if not, you have not added the right amount of tartaric acid, or perhaps your volume is not correct. You'll have to adjust your second addition accordingly.

If TA after the first half-addition is lower or higher than expected, it's best that you make use of my downloadable ACIDIFICATION CALCULATOR at ModernHomeWinemaking.com.

Likewise, if you are making red wine from grapes where, due to the presence of grape solids which don't constitute juice volume, you have to estimate the *volume of juice* to acidify. For this purpose, use the ACIDIFICATION CALCULATOR; it will walk you through the steps of determining the right amount of acid to add and also calculate a better estimate of juice volume.

Now! About adding tartaric acid ... wine will likely form tartrates and drop acidity (see sidebar on TARTARIC ACID AND TARTRATES on p. 77) resulting in a slightly lower final TA than your target. You may choose to leave it alone, or perhaps add a little more than calculated, say 10% more, to compensate for this drop in acidity.

EXAMPLE

Acidification with tartaric acid for the purpose of decreasing pH

You just crushed and pressed some 100 lbs (45 kg) of white grapes into about 6 gal (23 L) of juice, then taken a sample and measured 6.0 g/L TA and pH 3.80. TA is good but the pH is a bit high—you wish to reduce it to around 3.60 by adding tartaric acid.

Here you need to drop pH by about 0.2, so you figure you'll need maybe 2 g/L of tartaric acid. Calculate as follows the amount of tartaric acid to add:

$$\text{Total amount of tartaric acid to add (g)} = 2.0 \text{ g/L} \times 23 \text{ L}$$
$$= 46 \text{ g (about 3 tbsp)}$$

Start with 1 (one) tbsp to better gauge the impact on pH from adding tartaric acid. Add to the juice and mix thoroughly, and re-measure pH; you can measure pH right in the pail or carboy. Repeat with another tbsp, or perhaps switch over to tsp amounts and add smaller amounts and re-measure pH after each addition, and repeat until you hit your 3.60 pH target.

Great! But your TA has increased too. Potassium bitartrate will cause acidity to drop during fermentation, and then you'll also cold stabilize the wine, and those tartrates will cause acidity to drop further, all the while pH now remaining within a comfortable range.

If you are making red wine from grapes where you have to estimate the volume of juice to acidify, download the ACIDIFICATION CALCULATOR at ModernHomeWinemaking.com; it will walk you through the steps of determining the right amount of acid to add and also calculate a better estimate of juice volume.

Deacidification

When acidity is too high or pH is too low, you can reduce or "change" an acid to decrease acidity—this is referred to as deacidification. Since grape juice comprises mainly tartaric and malic acids, these are the acids you'll target.

You can reduce tartaric acid using an additive or by what is called cold stabilization, often referred to as cold crashing in home winemaking.

As for malic acid, you can reduce it by microbiological means using an appropriate yeast for the alcoholic fermentation. In conjunction with this method, or alternatively, you can "change" or transform all of the malic acid into the weaker lactic acid by putting the wine through malolactic fermentation (MLF)—the net result is a reduction in acidity.

How do you know if you have high amounts of malic acid? It's an educated guess. If you measure high acidity, when TA starts exceeding 8 g/L, for example, and you know grapes come from a cool or cold climate or perhaps from a poor vintage, then you can assume that there is a substantial amount of malic acid.

Of course, you always have the options of blending or ameliorating (adding water) to lower acidity.

Deacidification: Reducing tartaric acid using additives

To lower acidity by reducing tartaric acid, you have the choice of three additives, referred to as carbonate salts by chemists, which you'll find at your local home winemaking supply store: potassium carbonate, potassium bicarbonate and calcium carbonate. Lower amounts of potassium carbonate are needed, and so it's often the preferred additive, whereas calcium carbonate can leave an unappealing "chalky" taste if used excessively.

All three salts produce a lot of foaming that can cause some wine loss from spillage if you're not careful. Plan accordingly to avoid making a mess in your winemaking area. Carry out deacidification in a large container, for example, transferring your batch back into a pail to give you a bit more capacity, or, alternatively, deacidify just a portion of the batch, say, half, and then add that treated portion to the rest of the juice (or wine).

There's another important consideration with regards to foaming: it can cause the loss of precious aromas that you've work so hard to get. Deacidify in juice—as opposed to in wine—where aromas are to a large extent either "bound" or not yet created as there has been no fermentation.

Table 5.4 lists the amount of each carbonate salt needed to reduce TA by approximately 1 g/L in tartaric acid equivalents.

Be forewarned though! Deacidification chemistry is quite complex, and theory and practice seldom match—there can be significant differences.

Table 5.4: Amounts of carbonate salts needed to decrease TA by 1.0 g/L in tartaric acid equivalents

Carbonate salt	Amount (g/L)
Potassium carbonate	0.46
Potassium bicarbonate	0.67
Calcium carbonate	0.67

It's not straightforward. Use the recommended rates in Table 5.4, and use the half-addition method by adjusting the second addition accordingly until you hit your desired results.

To treat juice (or wine), first set the pail or carboy of juice in as cold an area as possible and allow to chill; this is to minimize foaming. Add your choice of carbonate salt and stir gently but thoroughly. Gently stir periodically over several hours making sure to place the lid or airlock back on the pail or carboy after each stir; the juice is protected in the headspace due to carbon dioxide gas generated from the reaction. Then rack the juice back into the pail or carboy.

Let's take a look at an example.

EXAMPLE

Deacidification with potassium carbonate

You just crushed and pressed some 100 lbs (45 kg) of white grapes into about 6 gal (23 L) of juice, then taken a sample and measured a TA of 8.0 g/L and a pH of 3.35.

You want to decrease TA by 2.0 g/L to around 6.0 g/L so as not to make an overly acidic wine and having to add sugar to balance the acidity. We'll use potassium carbonate to deacidify; the amount to add to the batch is calculated as follows:

$$\text{Total amount of potassium carbonate to add (g)} = 2.0\,\text{g/L} \times 23\,\text{L} \times 0.46$$
$$= 21\,\text{g (about 1 tbsp)}$$

Transfer the juice to a pail (if in a carboy) to handle the foaming, <u>add half that amount</u> of potassium carbonate to the juice, so about 10 g (½ tbsp), mix thoroughly, and allow the reaction to occur until there is no more gas produced. Take a new sample and re-measure TA and pH. Your TA should now be around 7 g/L, more or less, and your pH should have increased to 3.4 or 3.5.

Add the remaining potassium carbonate and repeat the process. Your TA should now be around 6 g/L, more or less, and your pH should have increased to 3.5 or 3.6.

If TA after the first half-addition is lower or higher than expected, use the downloadable DEACIDIFICATION CALCULATOR at <u>ModernHome Winemaking.com</u>.

Likewise, if you are making red wine from grapes where you have to estimate the volume of juice to deacidify, use the DEACIDIFICATION CALCULATOR; it will walk you through the steps of determining the right amount of carbonate salt to add and also calculate a better estimate of juice volume.

Deacidification: Reducing tartaric acid by cold crashing

Cold crashing is more of a "natural" technique for lowering acidity by reducing tartaric acid; it does not require the use of additives, just cold temperatures, however, it can only be performed in wine as it works only in the presence of alcohol. It can be easily performed in small-scale home winemaking by storing the carboy of wine in a refrigerator (typically set at around 40°F or 4°C) for about two weeks, though four weeks gives greater confidence.

The only caveat with this technique is that of predicting the drop in TA (and change in pH)—it's guesswork. As a rough guideline, you can expect a drop of 1 g/L TA, and pH to go up or down by about 0.1.

Deacidification: Reducing malic acid by microbiological means

You can reduce malic acid during alcoholic fermentation using a yeast known to degrade some amount of malic acid, or transform the acid completely through malolactic fermentation (MLF) by either relying on indigenous malolactic bacteria or introducing cultured bacteria. Since you don't know the amount of malic acid present in juice, you cannot predict the impact on TA, however, these deacidification techniques will prove useful when dealing with, for example, unaltered juice or grapes from a poor vintage or from cool- or cold-climate grape-growing regions from which you can expect substantial amounts of malic acid.

Lalvin 71B-1122 is one such yeast packaged in 5-g packets suitable for small batches; it can metabolize 20%–40% of the malic acid into small amounts of ethanol, or water and carbon dioxide gas depending on fermentation conditions—*it is not a conversion of malic acid into lactic acid* as with malolactic fermentation.

The conversion of malic acid into lactic acid is known as malolactic fermentation, or MLF, and although it reduces TA (and increases pH), the decision to carry out this conversion is really based on a desired style. Malolactic fermentation is described in Chapter SEVEN.

Deacidification: Through blending or amelioration

You can also lower acidity by blending or by ameliorating.

Blending is an effective technique for reducing—and also increasing—acidity in juice or wine where a high-TA juice or wine in need of acid reduction is blended with a low-TA juice or wine. Of course this technique depends on having blending components on hand; it may not be possible, for example, if you have harvested high-TA grapes and you have no other low-TA grapes coming in or you want to preserve varietal character and not blend in another variety.

Here too you can use the Pearson Square to determine TA of a blend. Note, however, that you cannot use the Person Square to determine pH of a blend as pH is a logarithmic function, and the Pearson Square only works for linear relationships.

Let's look at an example.

EXAMPLE

Pearson Square – blending two wines to lower TA

You have a 5-gal (19-L) batch of high-acid Baco Noir wine with a TA of 9.0 g/L (this is the B value) that you would like to lower to around 6.5 g/L (this is the C value) using Chambourcin wine with a TA of 5.0 g/L (this is the A value). Determine as follows how much Chambourcin you need to add to the Baco Noir to achieve the desired TA:

$$
\begin{array}{|c c|}
\hline
5.0 \qquad 2.5 \\
\\
6.5 \\
\\
9.0 \qquad 1.5 \\
\hline
\end{array}
$$

The Pearson Square says that you need 2.5 parts of Chambourcin wine for 1.5 parts of Baco Noir wine, or:

$$Volume\ of\ Chambourcin\ needed\ (gal) = 5\,gal \times \frac{2.5}{1.5} = 8.3\,gal$$

So you need to add 8.3 gal (31.4 L) of Chambourcin to 5 gal (19 L) of Baco Noir to lower acidity from 9.0 g/L to 6.5 g/L! This example illustrates that blending may require a significant amount of the second wine, which can definitely alter the character of the original wine.

Amelioration is not highly recommended as significant amounts of water too may be needed to reduce acidity, and that would dilute everything else, including SG, PA, and aromas and flavors, in the juice and wine. For example, you would need about 1.9 gal (7.2 L) of water to lower TA from 9.0 to 6.5 g/L in 5 gal (19 L) of juice or wine in the example above—that's a lot of water; more than a third as much juice!

Amelioration does not impact pH much, if at all, depending on the amount of water.

If you ameliorate, use the Pearson Square to figure out how much water to add; simply set the acidity of water to zero.

SULFUR DIOXIDE

Sulfur dioxide (SO_2) has long been used in winemaking as a sanitizing agent (see the section SANITIZING in Chapter THREE) but more importantly as a preservative against oxidative and microbial spoilages and aroma loss.

As a novice winemaker, if you want to use sulfur dioxide in your wines but you don't want to get into the chemistry and analysis of SO_2 and have to invest in the necessary equipment to measure SO_2, you can certainly make great wines, adequately protected against possible faults or spoilages, by making small periodic adjustments. You'll only need to learn the basics so that you have some practical knowledge and the confidence that your wines are always well protected. Again, as (if) your hobby grows and you become more comfortable with some of the basic chemistry and analytical tools, you can consult *Modern Home Winemaking* for a deeper dive.

You'll often hear the terms SO_2, free SO_2 and sulfite used interchangeably, which, technically, mean different things. Let's clear that up first.

SO_2 is the actual active form protecting wine. It exists in two forms in wine: as a gas in tiny amounts that protect against microbes; and in its ionized form, referred to as sulfite, which protects against chemical spoilage-type problems, namely, oxidation. The combination of SO_2 in its gas and sulfite forms is referred to as free SO_2, the parameter that is routinely measured and adjusted in winemaking. Free SO_2 is reported in mg/L or parts per million (ppm)—these units are equivalent.

But sulfite as well as metabisulfite are also used to refer to the crystalline powder, Campden tablets, or self-dissolving tablet forms, which are incorporated into wine to add SO_2. Potassium metabisulfite, or KMS, is a specific and the most common form used as a preservative. Metabisulfite is also available as sodium metabisulfite, but winemakers prefer the potassium form when used as a preservative so as to limit the amount of sodium added to wine, however small that may be.

When KMS is added to wine, it generates SO_2 and sulfite, i.e., free SO_2, as it dissolves. But free SO_2 diminishes over time as it reacts with other substances in wine. Oxygen consumes some free SO_2 and then reacts with other substances when free SO_2 becomes depleted and causes undesirable changes and spoilages; some spoilage microbes also thrive when oxygen is available and more so at higher pH. These are the reasons why wine must be protected from air, which is 21% oxygen, and spoilage microbes.

You therefore need to replenish and maintain an adequate level of free SO_2 throughout the life of the wine.

Since you are not measuring SO_2 levels, not yet, add the following amounts of KMS powder **per 5-gal (19-L) carboy:**

- ¼ tsp after the completion of alcoholic fermentation (see Chapter SIX) and malolactic fermentation (see Chapter SEVEN), if this last one is carried out;
- ⅛ tsp every 3 months thereafter, during aging; and
- ⅛ tsp after any operation that causes large amounts of oxygen to be absorbed, for example, after racking and filtering.

KMS addition instructions throughout this guide are given in tsp of KMS powder. If you prefer to use Campden tablets, refer to Table 5.5 for equivalent amounts to use per 5-gal (19-L) carboy, and how much free SO_2 is added approximately. Be sure to crush tablets to a fine powder.

KMS does not dissolve all that well in wine, so first dissolve in a little bit of cool tap water, then introduce into the wine and stir gently but thoroughly.

¼ tsp KMS adds roughly 50 ppm of free SO_2. This may be more SO_2 than you need, especially at low pH, but you won't know how much to add unless you know the pH *and* how much free SO_2 is in the wine, but this is fine and it won't add too much SO_2 if you follow the racking and processing guidelines recommended in this guide and assuming you'll bottle wine within 12 to 18 months.

Table 5.5: KMS powder and Campden tablets per 5-gal (19-L) carboy, and rough amounts of free SO_2 added

KMS powder	Campden tablets	Free SO_2 added (ppm)[1]
⅛ tsp	2	25
¼ tsp	4	50
½ tsp	8	100

[1]Based on a measurement of approximately 7.5 g for 1 tsp of KMS powder.

When you graduate to measuring free SO_2 in working with larger batches and aging reds for longer periods of time, you can use the downloadable SO2 CALCULATOR at ModernHomeWinemaking.com to help you with the calculations for adding more accurate amounts, and only as needed based on pH and amount of free SO_2 measured. You'll find that using a 10% KMS solution is much easier and more expedient when working with larger, numerous batches. You'll find instructions for preparing a 10% KMS solution in the SO2 CALCULATOR.

CHAPTER SIX

Fermentation—Transforming Grapes into Wine

*A*lcoholic fermentation is the transformation of fermentable sugars—glucose and fructose—by yeast into ethanol (ethyl alcohol) and vast amounts of carbon dioxide (CO_2) gas as the main products. Fermentation also produces a myriad of substances that give wine a multitude of aromas and flavors.

You can certainly try making natural wine, and hope that indigenous yeasts kick in and do a good job of completely fermenting sugars and producing favorable results. This can however be risky as you won't know what yeasts are present. These may not be able to ferment to typical wine alcohol levels, and may also produce undesirable results. You'll obtain much more predictable results using cultured *Saccharomyces cerevisiae* (abbreviated to *S. cerevisiae*) yeast, which you can select to match specific grape varieties and wine style objectives. Cultured yeast can withstand the harsh conditions of increasing alcohol and ferment to 16% ABV with some strains capable of reaching 18% ABV while performing consistently.

This chapter guides you in choosing an appropriate yeast, how to prepare yeast and manage nutrients for a trouble-free fermentation, and how to restart a stuck fermentation on the odd chance it happens.

CHOOSING WINE YEAST

You'll make much better wine, with greater aroma and flavor complexities, if you choose an appropriate yeast. Select one best adapted to the grape variety at hand and which is capable of handling fermentation challenges, such as high-SG/PA juice, or if fermenting in a colder area.

For making standard, carboy-sized batches of wine, cultured (active) dry yeast is available in 5-g packets, and cultured liquid yeast in 35-mL and 125-mL formats although the selection is more limited. The major producers of yeast products for making small batches include: Lalvin (Lallemand), Red Star (Fermentis), White Labs, and Wyeast Laboratories. Their products and specifications are listed at the end of this chapter.

 Dry yeast is more stable than liquid yeast. Dry yeast packets can be stored in a dry, cool area unopened for 12 to 18 months or for up to 6 months in a refrigerator once opened. Liquid cultures should be stored in a refrigerator and used within 6 months; the whole pack must be used once opened.

There are many, many more kinds (strains) of yeasts for bigger batches, but these are packaged in formats generally too big for small-scale winemaking. Check with your local suppliers as some may repackage large formats into smaller ones for hobbyists.

When choosing a suitable yeast strain, the most important decision factors are: grape variety, desired style of wine, alcohol range, and fermentation temperature.

Specific yeast strains are better adapted to specific grape varieties to produce the kinds of aromas and flavors you would expect from those wines. You cannot expect a yeast strain meant for making highly aromatic Moscato (white) wine to do wonders with a full-bodied Cabernet. Consult the yeast charts at the end of this chapter and pick a strain recommended for your grape variety. Remember to only use high-powered strains, such as Lalvin EC-1118 and Red Star Premier Blanc (formerly Pasteur Champagne), for difficult or stuck fermentations as these strains are fairly neutral otherwise and do not have much aromatic and taste impacts.

Check the yeast strain's nutritional requirements as each needs different amounts of nutrients to ferment successfully to dryness. Nutrition and when and how to add nutrients are discussed in more detail in the section WHICH, WHEN AND HOW MUCH NUTRIENTS TO USE below.

Next, check the strain's alcohol tolerance and temperature range. If you use a strain outside recommended ranges, you may cause undue stress and run a high risk of a sluggish or stuck fermentation and possibly undesirable aromas and flavors. A classic example would be hydrogen sulfide (H_2S), which imparts an unappealing rotten-egg smell. If you are dealing with high-SG/PA juice or grapes, consider ameliorating (adding water) to bring SG/PA to within working range of the yeast strain, otherwise, you'll need to use a high-powered strain. If you are dealing with fruit in poor condition, choose a fast-fermenting yeast strain so that it will out-compete microbial spoilers and won't contribute to acetic acid and volatile acidity (VA).

If you intend to process your wine for malolactic fermentation (MLF), which you'll learn all about in Chapter SEVEN, choose a strain that is more compatible with malolactic bacteria and MLF. If you are dealing with juice or grapes which you believe contain high amounts of malic acid (see *Deacidification* in the section ACIDITY AND PH on p. 85 in Chapter FIVE), go with a malic-degrading yeast, such as Lalvin 71B-1112, especially if you don't intend to put the wine through MLF for stylistic reasons.

Also look for any potential red flags in yeast specification charts. For example, some strains produce high levels of undesirable hydrogen sulfide (H_2S), such as Red Star's Premier Classique (formerly Montrachet) strain. If you have had H_2S problems in the past, try any of the so-called "no-H_2S" or "H_2S-preventing" yeast strains, although these may only be available in large formats.

As tempting as it might be, do *not* use two different yeast strains for fermenting the same batch in the hope of benefiting from the positive characteristics of each strain—the two strains may produce aromas or flavors that are not necessarily compatible. Both strains will perform suboptimally as they will compete for sugar and nutrients and likely not produce the desired results. Instead, split the batch into two and ferment each with the desired strain, then see how each turns out and blend the wines as desired.

Although they are sometimes used by home winemakers, bakers and bread yeasts are not recommended for making quality wine. As we have seen above, fermentation is much more than simply converting sugar into alcohol. These yeasts can generally ferment to a maximum of 8–10% alcohol. Also they do not produce the kinds of aromas and flavors that wine yeasts do, and often, they tend to leave a yeasty taste. They may also impact color extraction and stability in reds, and can be difficult to clarify as they tend to leave finer particles in suspension, which will require a much longer period to settle.

WHICH, WHEN AND HOW MUCH NUTRIENTS TO USE

Yeast needs plenty of micronutrients for its growth and metabolism to carry out fermentation successfully in what is a relatively hostile environment of high sugar followed by increasing alcohol. Micronutrients include nitrogen, the most essential, minerals (trace elements), vitamins, and sterols. Remember: The greater the amount of sugars in the juice or grapes, the greater the nutritional needs. Different strains also have different nutritional needs with some having a greater appetite than others. You'll find this bit of information on any yeast strain chart; it will say something like: LOW, MEDIUM or NORMAL, and HIGH.

A nutrient deficiency can cause fermentation problems and produce undesirable substances, which can impart very unappealing smells of rotten eggs, sewage, cooked cabbage, struck flint, and burnt rubber. As grapes are often deficient in nutrients, especially damaged or moldy fruit or grapes grown under poor conditions, you may need to supplement juice with more nutrients.

Excessive nutrients too can cause problems, not only with H_2S-related off-odors, but yeast may not necessarily consume all the nutrients, particularly if added late in the fermentation, which can result in leftover nutrients in the wine. If you later add sugar to sweeten the wine, residual yeast will feed on leftover nutrients and can kick-start a renewed fermentation. Spoilage microorganisms too can go after those nutrients.

There are many commercial preparations for adding nutrients, and you need to know which best to use and when to add. There are rehydration nutrients, yeast nutrients, and diammonium phosphate (DAP).

Rehydration nutrients "condition" and help protect yeast so that it adapts more readily with less risk of problems once introduced into juice (must). Always add *rehydration nutrients*, something like Go-Ferm (Lallemand) or Superstart (Laffort), to yeast when rehydrating dry yeast.

Never use DAP for rehydrating yeast—it is lethal at this stage. The section CONDUCTING AND MONITORING FERMENTATION below gives specific instructions on adding rehydration nutrients when preparing yeast.

Yeast nutrients (also referred to as complex nutrients and fermentation nutrients) are added to must and fermenting wine at two key points to replenish depleted nutrients. Fermaid K and Fermaid O (Lallemand), Nutristart (Laffort), and Superfood (BSG) are examples of yeast nutrient products. Do not interchange rehydration nutrients and yeast nutrients.

The first addition of yeast nutrients is done shortly after yeast inoculation, within 6–12 hours, to make sure yeast has sufficient nutrients to grow. Inoculation refers to the action of adding or "pitching" yeast to juice (must) to start fermentation. As these nutrients can be quickly consumed, you need to add more. This second addition is done when about one-third of sugars—the equivalent to a SG drop of about 30 to 35 points in most cases—has been metabolized.

Add yeast nutrients at the rate indicated on your product's packaging; it will generally be about 2 tsp for a standard carboy. Instructions will usually indicate a range; choose a rate at the lower end of the range for yeast with low nutrients needs, a mid-range rate for yeast with medium or normal needs, and a rate at the higher end of the range for yeast with high nutrients needs or if working with high-SG juice. This amount is divided evenly between the two additions.

Diammonium phosphate, or DAP, is often used because it delivers high amounts of (inorganic) nitrogen for a quick nutrient boost; however, it has lesser amounts of other beneficial nutrients and should therefore be used in combination with complex nutrients. DAP is also used as a yeast energizer in conjunction with yeast hulls for reviving a sluggish or stuck fermentation. Yeast hulls are purified yeast cell walls, rich in sterols and fatty acids, which absorb toxic substances that may inhibit yeast cell functions.

For organic winemaking, you'll find commercial nutrient preparations that contain organic nitrogen, that is, no DAP, no inorganic nitrogen, with no added vitamins and minerals.

CONDUCTING AND MONITORING FERMENTATION

Conducting fermentation to ensure it completes successfully to dryness involves preparing cultured yeast, inoculating or adding yeast to the juice, supplementing the juice with nutrients, managing fermentation temperature, and monitoring fermentation progress. If making natural wine and relying on indigenous yeast, you'll just need to wait until it kicks in on its own accord.

Adjusting Temperature

Before you inoculate the juice or are ready to let indigenous yeast jump into action, make sure that the juice is just below the desired fermentation temperature for the style of wine you want to create. As fermentation takes off, there will be an increase in temperature, possibly a sharp and significant increase, which may require cooling the fermentation. You'll need to be ready and able to swiftly adjust temperature to within the desired range.

To raise temperature, it may simply be a matter of raising room temperature and then dialing it back once fermentation becomes vigorous, or if you are working with a pail or carboy, you can wrap it with a heating belt.

It may be trickier to lower temperature depending on how much you need to reduce it. You can try lowering room temperature, moving the pail or carboy to a cooler area, or perhaps placing the pail or carboy in a cool- or cold-water bath.

Preparing the Yeast Culture and Inoculating the Juice

If inoculating with liquid yeast, follow the manufacturer's instructions.

If inoculating with cultured dry yeast, it's always best to first rehydrate the yeast with appropriate rehydration nutrients to help the yeast build up critical biomass. Some winemakers simply sprinkle yeast pellets on the surface of the juice or crushed grape solids, but this is a bit risky and can cause fermentation problems. A 5-g packet is good for a standard 5- or 6-gal (19- or 23-L) batch. Add another half pack or even a full one if you are working with high-SG juice, say, over 1.110, or when making red wine where it's best to use the total volume of juice plus grape solids, not just the estimated juice volume.

Rehydrate cultured dry yeast as shown in Figure 6.1. First add rehydration nutrients per manufacturer's instructions to fresh, chlorine-free water at around 110°F (43°C) in a sanitized measuring cup. For example, if using Go-Ferm rehydration nutrients, you need about one rounded teaspoon. Dissolve the powder very slowly (it doesn't dissolve easily) in about 100 mL of water. *Do not* use distilled or demineralized water as it may inhibit or kill yeast because of mineral deficiency.

Let the water with rehydration nutrients drop to around 105°F (40°C), then add the yeast pellets while stirring *very gently* with a sanitized spoon. Let hydrate for about 20 minutes; never exceed 30 minutes. At this point the yeast–nutrient solution, now called inoculum or yeast starter, should be foaming, more or less, depending on strain. Stir thoroughly but gently—there should be no clumps.

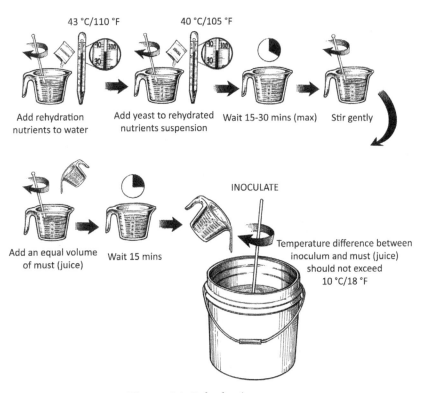

Figure 6.1: Rehydrating yeast

If working with juice at room temperature, you can add the inoculum to the juice directly, but if you are working at cooler cellar temperature, acclimate the yeast before inoculating the entire batch so as not to shock the yeast, which could cause fermentation problems. The difference in temperature between the juice and inoculum should not exceed 18°F (10°C). If necessary, add an equal volume of juice to the inoculum, let acclimate 15–20 minutes until it starts foaming. Repeat this process, doubling the volume each time, until the temperature difference is less than 18°F (10°C).

When ready, distribute the inoculum over the entire surface of the juice and stir thoroughly and vigorously to introduce oxygen to help yeast build biomass and grow. Place an airlock and bung if fermenting in a carboy or cover the pail (or whatever open-top fermentor you are using) with a lid or tarp to protect the juice (must) from the elements. For the airlock, simply pour in some water, vodka or sulfite solution to the fill-level lines (Figure 6.2), and place the protective cap on to keep dust out.

Within 6–12 hours after inoculation, do the first yeast nutrients addition as outlined in the section WHICH, WHEN AND HOW MUCH NUTRIENTS TO USE above.

Within 24–36 hours of inoculation, you should see signs of yeast activity; there should be bubbles forming at the edge and at the surface of the juice. If using an airlock, you'll soon start seeing some bubbling through the liquid, and it will progressively become vigorous. Be sure to gently stir the juice while waiting for fermentation to start to not only provide necessary oxygen but also to avoid bacteria and other microorganisms from taking hold on the surface.

Figure 6.2: Filling the airlock. If using water or a sulfite solution, replace the liquid in the airlock every 3 months during post-fermentation aging.

Once a day, during fermentation, stir the wine, take a sample with your sanitized wine thief or gravy baster, measure SG, PA and temperature using your sanitized hydrometer, test cylinder and thermometer, and record the numbers in your log book. The difference in PA compared to your initial reading is the amount of alcohol produced thus far. During an active fermentation, you should see a steady decline in SG and increase in temperature initially as fermentation produces a lot of heat. Temperature will start to decrease later during fermentation, and that's okay. Also, it's okay to return samples to the pail or carboy so as not to waste juice or wine if you are properly sanitizing equipment.

This next step is critical; you'll need to add more nutrients when approximately one-third of sugars has been converted. Use the same rate and process as the first addition, or as per your product's instructions, being extra careful to stir gently.

 Do not add any additives in powder or crystalline form directly into an active fermentation in a carboy—it will cause a vigorous eruption that will spill out of the carboy and create a mess.

To determine the one-third sugar depletion point, take the decimal part (called points) of the starting SG, or OG, and divide by 3. For example, if the starting SG was 1.100, a one-third drop of the 100 points (the 100 part of 1.100) is about 33 points (let's call it 35 points for simplicity); and therefore, when SG has reached around 1.065 (i.e., 1.100 – 0.035), do the second nutrients addition.

Usually, you'll ferment wine to complete dryness in your pail, vat or carboy, i.e., when SG is 0.995 or lower, before transferring to another vessel. However, depending on the style of wine you are making, for example, if you want to limit tannin extraction when making red wine, press earlier with some varieties to limit extraction of less desirable flavors. Or, if you are following instructions provided in a kit or by your juice or grapes supplier, you can rack to a carboy before dryness, for example, when SG is between 1.010 and 1.020, where wine will be better protected from the elements until fermentation completes. Install an airlock and bung on the carboy. To avoid having the bung slip up, wipe dry both the mouth of the carboy and bung, then insert the bung with airlock.

Although the terminology is confusing and not accurate, home winemakers refer to that first phase of fermentation, until racking to another fermentor, as *primary fermentation*, and then the final phase of fermentation in the second fermentor as *secondary fermentation*. We adopt that terminology here as it is in common use. Also refer to the sidebar on HOW TO USE PRIMARY AND SECONDARY FERMENTORS on pp. 102–103.

HOW TO USE PRIMARY AND SECONDARY FERMENTORS

This guide provides instructions for making 5-gal (19-L) carboy batches of wine to get 25 bottles. This means that the final volume is 5 gallons (19 liters) of ready-to-bottle wine. You'll need to keep that carboy full and exclude air to protect wine from oxidative spoilage during aging.

To get to that final volume, you need to start with a slightly greater volume because there will be losses when racking wine off its layer of sediment after fermentation and clarification. The extra amount needed depends on whether you are using juice or grapes. Losses are greater when using grapes because of the extra solids that precipitate and which need to be removed. You'll want some extra headspace, about 20% more, during primary fermentation to allow for foaming, lest you create a big mess in your winemaking area. Therefore, you'll need a primary fermentor bigger than the 5-gal (19-L) carboy in which wine will ultimately age.

You can use a 6-gal (23-L) pail or carboy as primary fermentor when making wine from juice or kit, or a 7.9-gal (30-L) pail when making wine from juice or kit supplied with a pack of grape skins, and a larger vat, something around 13 gal (50 L), for making wine from grapes. If you use a 6-gal (23-L) carboy as a primary fermentor, never fill above the shoulder height (the part where the carboy shape starts curving up), especially if you are fermenting at warmer temperatures, to avoid a volcano effect and wine spewing out of the carboy. A 6-gal (23-L) pail or carboy will also come in handy if you intend to degas 5-gal (19-L) batches of wine (see the section DEGASSING in Chapter EIGHT); you'll need the extra headspace to allow for foaming.

 Home winemakers typically use a pail with a loosely placed lid as primary fermentor believing that it provides plenty of beneficial oxygen to the wine, but that's not necessary. You can ferment whites and rosés, that is, all wines that do not involve macerating fruit, in carboys sealed with a bung and airlock. Ferment reds in a pail under a lid (or a vat covered with a tarp) when macerating fruit in juice and wine.

continued on next page

After primary fermentation, you can use a 5-gal (19-L) or 6-gal (23-L) carboy as secondary fermentor; the latter will have some head-space, but that's okay since there will still be some fermentation gas protecting wine from oxygen and spoilage microbes.

When fermentation is complete, rack the wine into a 5-gal (19-L) carboy. You have to keep that carboy properly topped up by making sure that the top of the wine level is within an inch of the stopper. You absolutely have to keep the carboy completely full and the wine pro-tected from here on. That means adding some wine, preferably the same or a similar wine, following a racking operation, for example, after the wine has clarified. You can use water if a similar wine is not available, but this inevitably causes some dilution.

The image below illustrates an example of how primary and sec-ondary fermentors are used when making red wine from fresh juice with a grape skins pack.

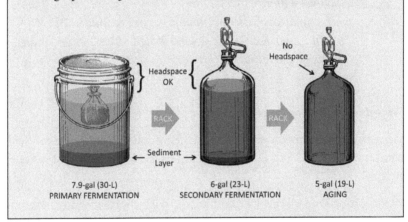

As you get close to the end of fermentation and bubbling activity slows down, a thick layer of dense, creamy sludge will have formed at the bottom of the pail or carboy. This sludge is referred to as the gross lees and con-tains primarily dead yeast cells, but also many other substances. If the wine is left in contact with these gross lees for more than a couple of days, the wine can develop some foul-smelling odors. As dead yeast cells break down in what is known as yeast autolysis, these start producing hydrogen sulfide (H_2S) and the familiar rotten-eggs smell. Rack the wine off the gross lees promptly, within 2–3 days from completion of fermentation to prevent issues, and similarly if fermentation is languishing and taking too long to complete.

Reds will receive one such racking when drawing the free-run wine and transferring the fermented grape solids to the press to extract press-run wine. As the press-run wine will still contain gross lees, rack again 24–36 hours later to a maximum of 3 days. Whatever precipitates from there on are fine lees, which still contain some small amounts of dead yeast cells but with no risk of causing off aromas. The fine lees also contain nitrogen-rich micronutrients that malolactic bacteria can utilize for malolactic fermentation, if you'll be doing an MLF.

In order to confirm the end of fermentation, the final SG should be 0.995 or lower with a steady reading for at least two consecutive days; do not rely on seeing no bubbling activity in the airlock—use your hydrometer.

 Always use a bung with an airlock on a carboy, at least until the wine has released all its fermentation gas (see the section DEGASSING in Chapter EIGHT). A solid bung (with no airlock) can cause overpressure and the glass carboy to explode before the bung pops out.

Stopping an Active Fermentation

What if you want to stop an active fermentation to keep some residual natural sugars to make a lighter-bodied (less alcohol), off-dry or sweeter style of wine?

The process is a bit involved and tricky, so it's always recommended to ferment completely dry and then sweeten to your desired taste as a better alternative (see SWEETENING: BALANCING ACIDITY AND SWEETNESS in Chapter TEN). If you want to halt fermentation to get lower alcohol, you can always ameliorate (add water to) the juice at the beginning, then ferment dry and sweeten to taste.

If you still want to stop an active fermentation, rack the wine just a touch over your desired final SG into a carboy, and transfer to a refrigerator. You won't be able to stop fermentation dead-on your desired SG as stoppage is not immediate, so you have to initiate the process at a slightly higher SG.

The next day, dissolve 1 (one) tsp of sulfite powder in a bit of water and stir this into the carboy. Let it chill for a few days, then take the carboy out and let the wine warm up to room temperature. Rack the wine to another carboy, rinse the first carboy with water, and coarse filter the wine back into the first carboy. Then filter again using medium pads back into the other carboy. One final filtration using fine filter pads is recommended, but this is optional. If using Buon Vino filter pads, coarse, medium and fine filter pads correspond to No. 1, No. 2 and No. 3, respectively. Chapter TWELVE describes the filtering process in detail.

You'll likely need to top up your carboy as you'll have some loss from racking and filtering. Measure SG to see how close you got to your desired SG. And lastly, add ¼ tsp of sulfite powder and one level tsp of potassium sorbate, each pre-dissolved in water. Stir well after each addition. This process will prevent any renewed fermentation as long as you maintain an adequate SO_2 level during aging; ⅛ tsp KMS (potassium metabisulfite) or 2 Campden tablets per carboy every 3 months should do the trick.

 Potassium sorbate cannot be used to stop an active fermentation; it only inhibits a renewed fermentation after the wine has been properly stabilized.

WHAT IF FERMENTATION STOPS BEFORE IT COMPLETES?

Even when all conditions seemed perfect—healthy grapes with no rot or damage, you added lots of nutrients, maintained temperature within range, etc.—fermentation can stall unexpectedly and inexplicably, and leave you to wonder how it could have happened and now how best to revive it. When fermentation stalls, it is said to be sluggish if it is still fermenting but too slowly. It is said to be stuck if it has stopped altogether, when SG hasn't changed in 24 hours.

Be aware, it can be very difficult to restart a problem fermentation depending on the state and stage of the wine; the lower the SG, the more difficult it will be.

The first step in dealing with a sluggish or stuck fermentation is recognizing that you have a problem so that you can deal with it swiftly. Do not allow other spoilage microorganisms to establish themselves before you jump into action. If you've been tracking SG changes every day and there has been little or no progress, then you know you have a problem. If you decide to throw in the towel, do not bottle the wine as is, it will likely start refermenting in bottles, and then you'll have a bigger problem. It's best to try and get fermentation to complete to dryness, and, if not, add ¼ tsp of sulfite powder and one level tsp of potassium sorbate, each pre-dissolved in water, making sure to stir well after each addition.

First, increase the temperature to 70°F–80°F (20°C–25°C), stir the wine, and look for signs of renewed activity. If fermentation does not restart within 24 hours, then you need to "detoxify" the wine with yeast hulls to remove toxic substances that may impede a restart, and re-inoculate with a strong yeast starter using a high-powered strain, such as, Lalvin K1V-1116, Red Star Premier Cuvée or Premier Blanc, or Wyeast 4946.

Follow these instructions for treating a standard-size carboy, making sure to keep the wine in the temperature range 70°F–80°F (20°C–25°C) throughout this procedure. In the case of red wine fermenting in a pail or vat, transfer all the wine, including pressed wine, to a carboy and let settle for about a day.

Step 1: Carefully rack the wine off its lees and into a carboy; avoid splashing to limit oxygen uptake. Dissolve ⅛ tsp KMS in a little bit of cool water, and stir in gently. Add one rounded tsp of yeast hulls while stirring thoroughly but gently. Stir every 12 hours from here on.

Step 2: Withdraw about ½ gal (2 L) of wine and transfer to a large measuring cup or pitcher. Add 3 tbsp of table sugar and stir until well dissolved, then add just a pinch of DAP or complex yeast nutrients, such as Fermaid K or O.

Step 3: In a separate container that can hold at least 1 gal (4 L) of wine, prepare a yeast starter using a strong strain and rehydration nutrients as per instructions in the subsection *Preparing the Yeast Culture and Inoculating the Juice* in the section CONDUCTING AND MONITORING FERMENTATION on p. 98.

Once the yeast starter is ready, add about 200 mL of wine from the volume drawn in Step 2. This should start fermenting fairly quickly. Stir occasionally and let ferment *until the SG drops to 1.000.*

Now double the volume by adding about 400 mL of wine from the volume drawn in Step 2, and again, stir occasionally and let ferment until it becomes vigorous. Let subside and then double the volume again by adding the rest of the wine withdrawn in Step 2, let ferment until it becomes vigorous, then proceed to Step 4.

Step 4: Add the fermenting yeast starter to the batch of wine and stir thoroughly. Dissolve ½ tsp of complex nutrients in a little water and stir into the carboy. Place an airlock and bung on the carboy. The batch of wine should restart fermenting and finish at SG 0.995 or lower.

YEAST CHARTS BY MANUFACTURER

This section provides charts, by manufacturer, of the most popular wine-making yeast strains to make a standard, carboy-sized batch of wine. Charts also include key fermentation data including: temperature range, alcohol tolerance, nutrient needs, if strains can be used to restart a stuck fermentation, if these can be used to degrade malic acid relatively significantly, as well as types of wines and recommended grape varieties for each strain with red varieties identified in bold. Varieties are abbreviated as listed below under *Grape Variety Abbreviations*. Recommended varieties are based on a mix of manufacturer or vendor literature, and from input from amateur and commercial winemakers as well as from personal experience. Those identified as "Rosé" can be any red variety that can produce rosé wine.

You can use the downloadable worksheet at ModernHomeWinemaking.com to help you select a yeast strain for your desired grape variety and yeast manufacturer.

 The data presented in the following charts are believed to be correct and up to date at the time of publication. Data may change without prior notice due to, but not limited to, changes in manufacturer's specifications.

Grape Variety Abbreviations

WHITE VINIFERAS

AL = Albariño
AU = Auxerrois
CB = Chenin Blanc
CH = Chardonnay
GW = Gewürztraminer
MU = Muscat
PG = Pinot Gris
RI = Riesling
SB = Sauvignon Blanc
VI = Viognier

RED VINIFERAS

AB = Alicante Bouschet
AG = Aglianico
BB = Barbera
CF = Cabernet Franc
CM = Carménère
CS = Cabernet Sauvignon
GR = Grenache
GY = Gamay
MA = Malbec
ME = Merlot
MV = Mourvèdre
NB = Nebbiolo
PN = Pinot Noir
PS = Petite Sirah
PT = Pinotage
PV = Petit Verdot
SG = Sangiovese
SY = Syrah
TN = Touriga Nacional
TP = Tempranillo
ZF = Zinfandel

WHITE NON-VINIFERAS

CW = Cayuga White
LC = La Crescent
NI = Niagara
SN = Scuppernong
SV = Seyval Blanc
TR = Traminette
VB = Vidal Blanc

RED NON-VINIFERAS

BN = Baco Noir
CN = Chambourcin
CO = Concord
CT = Catawba
FR = Frontenac
LM = Léon Millot
MF = Maréchal Foch
MQ = Marquette
NR = Noiret
NT = Norton
SC = St. Croix

LALVIN

Yeast	Temp. range (°C)	Temp. range (°F)	Alcohol tolerance	Nutrient needs	Restart stuck ferm.[1]	Malic degradation	Types of wines			Recommended varieties[2,3]
							White	Rosé	Red	
71B-1122	15–29	59–84	14%	Low		★	★	★	★	AL, AU, BN, CN, CO, GY, LC, LM, MF, MQ, NI, NR, NT, PG, RI, FR, GR, SC, SV, VB, Rosé
BM4X4	18–28	64–82	16%	High			★		★	AG, CH, CN, CS, FR, GR, MQ, PS, PT, SG, ZF
EC-1118	10–30	50–86	18%	Low	★		★	★	★	All varieties
ICV-D47	15–28	59–82	15%	Low			★	★		CH, VI, Rosé
K1V-1116	10–35	50–95	18%	Med	★		★	★	★	CB, CW, VB, Rosé
QA23	15–32	59–90	16%	Low			★	★		AL, CB, CH, CW, GW, LC, MU, PG, RI, SB, SV, TR, VB, VI
RC 212	15–30	59–86	16%	Med					★	BN, CN, CS, FR, GR, GY, MF, MQ, PN

NOTES

[1] Can be used for all varieties.

[2] "Rosé" means any variety that can be used for making a rosé wine.

[3] Red varieties are identified in bold.

RED STAR

Yeast	Temp. range (°C)	Temp. range (°F)	Alcohol tolerance	Nutrient needs	Restart stuck ferm.[1]	Malic degradation	Types of wines			Recommended varieties[2,3]
							White	Rosé	Red	
Premier Rouge (Pasteur Red)	18–30	64–86	15%	High					★	**AG, BN, CF, CM, CN, CS, FR, GR, GV, LM, ME, MF, MV, NR, PN, PS, PT, PV, SC, SG, SY, TN, ZF**
Premier Classique (Montrachet)	14–30	57–86	15%	Low			★	★	★	**CH, CF, CS**, Rosé
Côte des Blancs	14–30	57–86	14%	High		★	★	★		AL, AU, CB, CH, GW, LC, MU, NI, RI, SB, SV, TR, VB, Rosé
Premier Blanc (Pasteur Champagne)	10–30	50–86	18%	Very Low	★	★	★	★	★	AL, AU, CB, CH, **CF, CS**, LC, MU SN, VI, Rosé
Premier Cuvée	10–30	50–86	16%	Very Low	★		★	★	★	**BN**, CH, **CS, CW, FR, LM, MF, MQ, NR, NT, SC, SV**, TR, VB, Rosé

NOTES

[1] Can be used for all varieties.

[2] "Rosé" means any variety that can be used for making a rosé wine.

[3] Red varieties are identified in bold.

WHITE LABS

Yeast	Temp. range (°C)	Temp. range (°F)	Alcohol tolerance	Nutrient needs	Restart stuck ferm.	Malic degradation	White	Rosé	Red	Recommended varieties[2,3]
California Pinot Noir (WLP707)	16–32	60–90	>15%	Med			★		★	CH, **CS, GY, PN**
Champagne (WLP715)	21–24	70–75	>15%	Med			★			AU, LC, VB, VI
Avize (WLP718)	16–32	60–90	15%	Med			★			CH
Sweet Wine (WLP720)	21–24	70–75	15%	Med			★	★		GW, MU, NI, RI, SN, Rosé
Steinberg-Geisenheim (WLP727)	10–32	50–90	15%	Med			★	★		GW, RI, Rosé
Chardonnay (WLP730)	10–32	50–90	15%	Med			★	★		AL, AU, CH, Rosé
French White (WLP735)	16–32	60–90	>15%	Med			★			CB, CW, SV, VI
Merlot Red (WLP740)	16–32	60–90	>15%	High			★		★	AG, BN, CH, CM, CN, CT, ME, PN, PS, PT, PV, SB, SC, SY, TN
Assmanshausen (WLP749)	10–32	50–90	>15%	Med			★	★	★	PN, RI, ZF, Rosé
French Red (WLP750)	16–32	60–90	>15%	Med			★		★	AG, CF, CM, CS, FR, LM, MA, ME, MF, MQ, MV, NR, NT, PS, PT, PV, SB, SC, TP
Cabernet Red (WLP760)	16–32	60–90	>15%	Med			★		★	BB, CF, CH, CM, CS, FR, GR, LM, MF, MQ, MV, NB, NR, NT, PV, SG, TP, ZF
Suremain Burgundy (WLP770)	16–32	60–90	>15%	High			★	★	★	BN, CH, CO, CT, GY, PN, SB, Rosé

NOTES

[1]Can be used for all varieties.

[2]"Rosé" means any variety that can be used for making a rosé wine.

[3]Red varieties are identified in bold.

WYEAST LABORATORIES

Yeast	Temp. range (°C)	Temp. range (°F)	Alcohol tolerance	Nutrient needs	Restart stuck ferm.[1]	Malic degradation	Types of wines			Recommended varieties[2,3]
							White	Rosé	Red	
Dry White/Sparkling (4021)	13–24	55–75	17%	Med			★		★	AU, CH, **CF**, CW, GW, LC, MU, PG, **PT**, SB, SV, TR
Red (4028)	13–32	55–90	14%	Med			★		★	AG, AL, **BB**, CB, **CF**, CH, **CM, CO, CS, CT, FR, GR, GY, LM, MA, ME, MQ, MV, NR, PN, PS, PV**, SB, **SC, SG**, SN, SV, **SY, TN, TP, ZF**, VI
Fruity White (4242)	13–24	55–75	12%	Med			★	★	★	CB, CH, CW, GW, GY, LC, MU, NI, PG, TR, Rosé
Italian Red (4244)	13–24	55–75	14%	Med					★	**BB, MA, NB, PV, SG, TP**
Summation Red (4267)	13–32	55–90	14%	Med			★		★	AG, **BB, BN, CF, CM, CO, CS, FR, LM, MA, ME, MQ, MV, NR**, PS, PV, **SB, SC, SG, SY, TP, VI**
Dry/Fortified (4767)	16–32	60–90	14%	Med			★		★	CB, CH, **ME**, MU, MV, **SG, TN, TP, ZF**
Sweet White (4783)	13–24	55–75	14%	Med			★			AL, AU, GW, RI, SN, SV, TR, VB
Bold Red/High Alcohol (4946)	16–29	60–85	18%	Med	★				★	AG, **BN, CN, CS, FR, LM, MF, MQ, PN, PS, PT, SY, TN, ZF**

NOTES

[1] Can be used for all varieties.

[2] "Rosé" means any variety that can be used for making a rosé wine.

[3] Red varieties are identified in bold.

CHAPTER SEVEN

Malolactic Fermentation — Softening a Wine's Acidity … and More

Malolactic fermentation, often referred to as malo or simply MLF, is the conversion of naturally occurring, sharper-tasting malic acid (think green apples) into the softer, weaker lactic acid (think dairy products) by indigenous or cultured malolactic bacteria (also re-ferred to as lactic acid bacteria). It is almost always desired in red wines to lower acidity for better balance with tannins. MLF also produces many other substances that enhance aromas and flavors. The drop in acidity and changes in aromas and flavors often don't work well in whites, with some exceptions, such as in a full-bodied, oak-style Chardonnay. This style of wine prefers less acidity and benefits from diacetyl, a uniquely favorable and well-known by-product of MLF that imparts an unmis-takable buttery aroma.

If you make wine from fresh juice but which has had sulfite added, it may contain sufficient sulfur dioxide (SO_2) to inhibit malolactic bacteria and MLF. MLF can be very difficult, perhaps impossible under these circumstances, therefore inquire about how much sul-fite was added or measure SO_2 if you can, and forego MLF if any significant amount was added—you'll save yourself a lot of grief.

If you make wine from kits, you can skip this chapter. Juice and concentrate in kits have been prepared to produce balanced wines. Putting kit wines through MLF can compromise quality and yield unexpected results that can be very different than the style the kit manufacturer intended.

CONDUCTING MALOLACTIC FERMENTATION

You can conduct MLF concurrently to overlap with alcoholic fermentation, or sequentially after it's completed. There are pros and cons for each method, and you'll come to adopt your own preference with experience.

 For brevity, we'll refer to "alcoholic fermentation" simply as "fermentation," unless a distinction is made. Malolactic fermentation will always be qualified as such and also referred to as MLF.

In the concurrent method, you initiate MLF at the same time as fermentation, or anytime between the start and end of fermentation. The idea here is to give malolactic bacteria a greater chance of success in carrying out malic acid conversion while the alcohol level is low and building up slowly, so that MLF completes ahead of or at the same time as fermentation. This short interval limits diacetyl production and any buttery-related aroma; this might be best if you are not partial to that style of wine. When fermentation and MLF are complete, you can immediately stabilize the wine with sulfite and move it to a cooler area for aging. A possible risk is that MLF may stall or perhaps does not complete before fermentation does for a variety of reasons, often because yeast and bacteria are competing for nutrients. It can be a challenge restarting a sluggish or stuck MLF. And if fermentation becomes stuck, MLF is jeopardized as you try and take actions to restart fermentation.

In the sequential method, you initiate MLF right after completion of fermentation so that each is separate and there is no competition for nutrients between yeast and bacteria. If you run into problems with fermentation, you can deal with restarting it without impacting MLF (which would not have started yet). But now malolactic bacteria have to perform in a more hostile environment because of the relatively high amount of alcohol, and that will likely prolong MLF. It can last weeks, perhaps months, all the while without sulfite protection and at relatively warm (room) temperature; it's not ideal. But if you want a full-bodied, buttered-up Chardonnay, a sequential MLF is the way to go as a longer MLF favors diacetyl production.

Again, you'll come to develop your own preference as to which method works best for you. Just keep in mind that, if making high-alcohol wines that start exceeding 14.5% ABV, you'll be challenged to complete MLF. A concurrent MLF might be best in this case.

Before initiating MLF, assess whether to expect more or less favorable conditions as those will play into what strain of bacteria to use. You can generally expect a more favorable MLF when ABV is below 15%, pH is greater than 3.2, and temperature is in the range 64°F–72°F (18°C–22°C). Also, if you are measuring SO_2, confirm that *total* SO_2 is no more than 40–60 mg/L; consult manufacturers' specifications at the end of this chapter for your malolactic bacterium. If you follow the winemaking instructions in this guide, excessive total SO_2 will not be an issue.

To conduct MLF, you can gamble using indigenous malolactic bacteria, although this is always risky, riskier than relying on indigenous yeast for fermentation given the greater proliferation of spoilage bacteria. It's generally preferred to inoculate with cultured malolactic bacteria that meet the criteria above. Unfortunately, there's only a limited selection of cultured dry bacteria for small batches; 2.5 g is the smallest pack you'll find, and that's good for up to 66 gal (250 L) of wine—that's thirteen carboys! And these 2.5-g packets don't come cheap. If you have many batches on the go, coordinate your winemaking to take full advantage of the pack, as once opened, you'll have to use it all as quickly as possible. Unless you have a good gram scale, it will be difficult to split 2.5 g of powder into tiny amounts per batch; simply rehydrate the whole pack in a measured amount of water, and then divvy that up for each batch using a graduated cylinder—it's so much easier. There are some liquid cultures available good for standard carboys, such as those from White Labs and Wyeast Laboratories; consult the malolactic bacterium charts at the end of this chapter.

 Freeze-dried culture packets can be stored for up to 18 months in the fridge at 40°F (4°C) or up to 36 months in the freezer at 0°F (−18°C) in their original sealed packaging. Use the entire packet as quickly as possible once opened. Store liquid cultures in the fridge and use within 6 months.

Maintain temperature in the range 64°F–72°F (18°C–22°C) during the MLF. If doing concurrent fermentation and MLF, malolactic bacteria will find sufficient nutrients to carry out malic acid conversion. If doing a sequential MLF, first rack the wine off the gross lees, then add malolactic nutrients, something like Opti-Malo Plus if you can find it in a small packet, just before initiating MLF. Then follow the product's instructions on how best to add bacteria. Some products can be added directly, with no preparation, while others may require rehydration in water, possibly using rehydration nutrients, such as Acti-ML. You will need 1 (one) tsp of Acti-ML per carboy. First dissolve the powder in about 50 mL of chlorine-free tap water at around 77°F (25°C). Add the required amount of bacterium culture, wait about 15 minutes, then add the hydrated culture to the juice or wine while stirring very gently. Put the airlock and bung back on if MLF is to be done in a carboy.

You should see (possibly with the use of a flashlight) tiny bubbles rising ever so slowly towards the surface of the wine in a carboy when MLF begins. It is otherwise not possible to ascertain that MLF has begun if done concurrently with fermentation as the latter generates a lot of foaming.

During a sequential MLF, you can stir the wine *very gently*—to avoid oxygen pickup—once or twice a week just to get the lees and bacterial cells back into suspension to favor a smoother and faster MLF.

To monitor MLF progress and to determine completion, you'll need to get acquainted with how to perform a paper chromatography test, described below.

When MLF is complete, promptly stabilize the wine with sulfite to protect against microbial spoilage. Either add sulfite without racking if you intend to age the wine further on the lees, or first rack then add sulfite. Dissolve ¼ tsp KMS (potassium metabisulfite) in cool water, and gently stir into the wine. Secure the carboy with an airlock and bung, and allow to age.

If you intend to sweeten to make an off-dry or sweeter style of wine, do *not* add sorbate if the wine has undergone MLF as malolactic bacteria will convert sorbate into a substance with an off-putting geranium-like smell. We'll deal with this case in Chapter NINE.

TESTING FOR MLF COMPLETION

MLF is considered complete when malic acid has been completely converted into lactic acid. Any remaining malic acid will make the wine unstable, meaning that MLF can spontaneously restart at a later time, perhaps in bottles, and cause spoilage.

Paper chromatography is the most common method used to test for MLF. It is relatively easy to run although it involves handling a very strong smelling solvent.

⚠ *Paper chromatography makes use of a strong and irritating solvent that requires extra handling care. Use in a well-ventilated area.*

The procedure involves "spotting" a special sheet of paper with a sample of each wine to be tested, and placing the paper in a jar with a small amount of the solvent. As the solvent is absorbed and travels up the paper, the different acids in the samples travel up, stopping at different levels depending on the chemical nature of each acid. After drying out, each acid creates a spot on the paper, and then you determine the presence or absence of each acid based on its expected position. *MLF is said to be complete when the malic acid spot disappears completely*; a lactic acid spot appears at the top.

To run the test, you'll need the following material and chemicals, which you can purchase as a kit (Figure 7.1) from your local winemaking supplier:

- Whatman #1 chromatography paper, approximately 7¼ in × 9 in (184 mm × 230 mm)
- 1-gal (4-L) wide-opening jar with a tight-closing lid
- Disposable capillary tubes
- Chromatography solvent (bright orange color)
- 3.0 g/L (0.3%) reference solutions for each acid (tartaric, malic and lactic)

And you'll need a small sample—a few mL—of each wine to be tested.

Using a *lead pencil* (not a pen as ink will run when absorbed by the solvent), draw a horizontal line on the long side of a sheet of Whatman paper about 1 inch (2.5 cm) from the bottom edge, as shown in Figure 7.2. Mark an X

Figure 7.1: Paper chromatography test kit

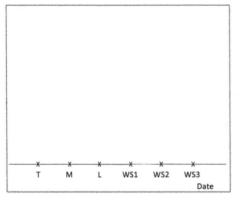

Figure 7.2: Spotting Whatman paper with acid standards and wine samples (WS) for running a paper chromatography test

for each acid reference and wine sample to be tested, spaced apart 1 inch (2.5 cm) with the first and last spots at least 1 inch (2.5 cm) away from each edge. Label each acid reference (e.g., T for tartaric, M for malic and L for lactic) and wine sample below each X with your pencil, and write the date of the test in the bottom corner.

Place the paper flat on a table and slide a pencil under the paper parallel to the drawn line, the idea being that the edge of the paper is slightly elevated off the table. You will be "spotting" the paper, i.e., placing tiny drops of acid or wine on the X marks, and you don't want the liquid on the underside touching the table.

Starting with the tartaric reference, draw a small sample using a capillary tube; place your index finger on top of the tube to prevent the sample from running out. Use a tissue paper to wipe off any excess at the bottom. Spot the X mark labeled "T" with one drop of tartaric acid reference solution being careful not to let the paper absorb too much liquid. Release your finger from the top and accurately spot again with three more drops. If drops don't overlap nicely or you use too much of the sample, the spots will become large and will make the analysis more difficult. Using a different capillary tube, repeat for each acid reference and wine sample making sure to apply the same exact number of drops, i.e., a total of four.

When done spotting all acid reference solutions and wine samples, let the spots dry for a few minutes, or use a hair dryer to speed up the drying.

Curl the paper into a perfect cylindrical shape along the short axis of the paper, making sure that there is no overlap—this is important—and then staple the edges of the paper at the top, middle and bottom.

Pour approximately 100 mL of chromatography solvent in the jar and insert the curled paper into the solvent (Figure 7.3). The line drawn on the paper should be just above the solvent level. Close the jar tightly with a lid, making sure that the curled paper remains perfectly vertical. Let stand until the solvent has reached the top of the paper; this will take about 3–4 hours. As the solvent travels up the paper, it will "drag" each acid up from reference solutions and wine samples, but you won't see anything just yet.

When the solvent has reached the top, open the jar, remove the paper and hang to dry using plastic clips in a warm, well-ventilated area or over a heat source (e.g., electrical baseboard).

Return the leftover solvent to its container and thoroughly rinse the jar with plenty of water and let dry.

 The solvent can be reused but will need to be replaced after 6 months, perhaps a year. If the spots don't develop clearly, if there is excessive streaking of spots, or if the paper remains yellowish and does not develop to a bluish color, replace the solvent.

At this point, there is nothing really visible on the paper; it will look kind of yellowish, orangey. Drying will take several hours, therefore plan on leaving the paper hanging overnight.

As the paper dries, it will turn a blue–green color with bright yellow spots corresponding to each acid. When dry, remove the staples and uncurl the paper, and analyze the results.

Using the yellow spots formed by each of the reference acids, you can see the component acids for each wine sample. Since all (grape) wines have tartaric acid, there will be a tartaric acid spot in each sample at the same height as the tartaric reference spot. For each sample, moving up the paper from its tartaric acid spot, look for the presence of a malic acid spot. If there is no visible sign of a yellow spot, it means that MLF has completed and converted all malic acid into lactic acid for that sample, and there-

Figure 7.3: Chromatography test (in a clear jar to show how paper is inserted)

fore, if you move up the paper for that sample, there should be a bright yellow spot at the same level as the lactic acid reference spot. The malic spot has to have *completely* disappeared to give you confidence that all malic acid has been converted. If you have trouble deciphering the presence (or absence) of spots, try holding the paper up against a strong light source.

Figure 7.4 depicts an example of a paper chromatography test illustrating separation of acids.

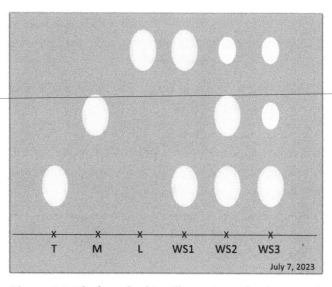

Figure 7.4: Black-and-white illustration of a theoretical chromatogram showing separation of acids in three wine samples, WS1, WS2, and WS3. MLF is complete in WS1 given the absence of a malic spot; MLF has likely not started in WS2 given the intensity of the malic spot and weak "lactic spot," but the latter is likely due to another acid, i.e., succinic acid, produced during alcoholic fermentation and which appears in approximately the same position as for lactic acid; and MLF has started and is in progress in WS3 given the lower intensity of the malic spot.

If MLF is complete, you can proceed with stabilization and add sulfite, but it is recommended letting the wine stand for another week or two to ensure that any residual malic acid that is not visible on the test is allowed to complete conversion. If there is even a slight hint of a yellow spot, then

MLF is not complete, and you should allow for more time; there will still be a lactic spot towards the top of the paper.

WHAT IF I CAN'T GET MLF TO COMPLETE?

Malolactic bacteria are finicky and very sensitive to their environment, i.e., pH, % ABV, SO_2, and temperature. Many things can cause MLF to become sluggish or stuck. If MLF is taking unusually long and the malic spot in the paper chromatography test is showing little or no progress, i.e., it is not fading and disappearing, then you need to try and restart MLF as it can be risky leaving the wine at room temperature without sulfite protection.

First assess the situation and your chances of success; if pH, % ABV and total SO_2 are outside the recommended range for your malolactic bacterium, it can be very difficult, perhaps impossible, to restart the MLF.

If you don't intend to take action to complete MLF, you'll need to stabilize the wine with sulfite and lysozyme, or chitosan, against the possibility of renewed MLF and spoilage (see the section RESIDUAL MALIC ACID in Chapter NINE).

If you decide to give it a go at restarting MLF, first try increasing temperature towards the higher end of the bacterium's specification, and look for signs of renewed activity. If MLF does not restart within 24–48 hours, try the following restart procedure for treating a 5-gal (19-L) carboy of wine; it is very similar to dealing with a problem fermentation, i.e., detoxification followed by re-inoculation with a stronger strain plus special nutrients, called MLF activator, such as ML Red Boost or MaloBoost.

Keep the wine in the range 64°F–72°F (18°C–22°C) throughout this procedure.

Step 1: Add one rounded tsp of yeast hulls to the wine while stirring thoroughly but gently to minimize oxygen uptake. Stir thoroughly every 6–12 hours for 48 hours, and then *gently* rack the wine off its lees and into another carboy, being careful not to splash the wine.

Step 2: Dissolve 1 (one) tsp of MLF activator in 50 mL of water or wine, then add to the wine and stir thoroughly but gently. Wait 24 hours before proceeding to the next step.

Step 3: Choose a strong malolactic bacterium strain, such as Lalvin MBR VP41 or Wyeast Er1A & Ey2d Blend. Choose a strain that is known to be good at restarting a stuck MLF. Prepare or add directly to the wine, as per product instructions, but at *double the normal rate* for the product used. Stir thoroughly but gently. Monitor progress using paper chromatography, and sulfite immediately when malic acid has been completely converted.

MALOLACTIC BACTERIUM CHARTS BY MANUFACTURER

This section provides charts, by manufacturer of the most popular wine-making malolactic bacterium strains along with key MLF data including: temperature range, alcohol tolerance, nutrient needs, minimum pH, maximum total SO_2, diacetyl production, if the strains can be used to restart a stuck MLF, and types of wines each can be used in.

Some freeze-dried malolactic bacterium cultures can be added directly to must or wine or first rehydrated; liquid cultures can be added directly to must or wine. Always follow the manufacturer's instructions.

 The data presented in the following charts are believed to be correct and up to date at the time of publication. Data may change without prior notice due to, but not limited to, changes in manufacturer's specifications.

LALLEMAND

Bacteria	Format	Addition method	Temp. range (°C)	Temp. range (°F)	Alcohol tolerance	Nutrient needs	Minimum pH	Maximum Total SO$_2$ (mg/L)	Diacetyl production	Restart stuck MLF	Types of wines		
											White	Rosé	Red
Enoferm Beta	Freeze-dried	Direct	14–27	57–81	15%	High	3.2	60	Seq.: High Co-inoc: Low		★	★	★
Lalvin MBR 31	Freeze-dried	Direct	13–28	55–82	14%	Med	3.1	45	High		★	★	★
Lalvin MBR VP41	Freeze-dried	Direct	16–28	61–82	16%	Low	3.1	60	Low	★	★	★	★
PN4	Freeze-dried	Direct	16–28	61–82	16%	Med	3.1	60	High				★
ML Prime	Freeze-dried	Direct	20–26	68–79	10%	Very Low	3.4	50	Very Low				★

WHITE LABS

Bacteria	Format	Addition method	Temp. range (°C)	Temp. range (°F)	Alcohol tolerance	Nutrient needs	Minimum pH	Maximum Total SO$_2$ (mg/L)	Diacetyl production	Restart stuck MLF	Types of wines		
											White	Rosé	Red
WLP675	Liquid	Direct	13–24	55–75	15%	Low	White: 3.1 Red: 3.3	40	Low		★	★	★

WYEAST LABORATORIES

Bacteria	Format	Addition method	Temp. range (°C)	Temp. range (°F)	Alcohol tolerance	Nutrient needs	Minimum pH	Maximum Total SO$_2$ (mg/L)	Diacetyl production	Restart stuck MLF	Types of wines White	Rosé	Red
Er1A (4114)	Liquid	Direct	21–32	70–90	>12%	N/R[1]	3.4[2]	50	no data				★
Ey2d (4221)	Liquid	Direct	13–24	55–75	>12%	N/R[1]	3.4[2]	50	no data		★	★	
Er1A & Ey2d Blend (4007)	Liquid	Direct	13–32	55–90	>12%	N/R[1]	3.4[2]	50	no data	★	★	★	★

[1] None required.
[2] Time to complete MLF is less than 1 month at pH>3.4 at 18°C (64°F).
At pH<3.3, time to complete MLF for Er1A, Ey2d and Blend are 1-2 months, 2-3 months, and 1-3 months, respectively.

CHR HANSEN

Bacteria	Format	Addition method	Temp. range (°C)	Temp. range (°F)	Alcohol tolerance	Nutrient needs	Minimum pH	Maximum Total SO$_2$ (mg/L)	Diacetyl production	Restart stuck MLF	Types of wines White	Rosé	Red
Viniflora CH16	Freeze-dried	Direct	17–25	63–77	16	Low	3.4	40	Med				★
Viniflora CH35	Freeze-dried	Direct	15–25	59–77	14	Low	3.1	45	High	★	★	★	★
Viniflora Oenos	Freeze-dried	Direct	17–25	63–77	14	Low	3.2	40	Med		★	★	★

CHAPTER EIGHT

Fining Wine to a Bright, Smooth Finish

O nce fermentation is complete, including malolactic fermentation (MLF) if carried out, wine is clarified either naturally or with the use of processing aids known as *clarifying agents* or *fining agents*. This part of the winemaking process is referred to as *clarification* or *fining*, although the latter term has a slightly different meaning as we'll see below.

Wine can become perfectly clear with no special treatment other than giving it time for suspended particles to settle and form a layer at the bottom of the carboy. The wine is then separated, or *racked*, from that layer of sediment.

If you're looking to bottle your batch within just a few weeks or months, it will likely not clear sufficiently quickly on its own; you may need to degas the wine and treat it with a clarifying agent, and possibly filter it. Even after a long time aging in carboy, a wine may not clear naturally. You'll need to determine the cause and you may have no choice but to use a clarifying agent. Sometimes, a perfectly clear wine may unexpectedly become cloudy or form deposits, possibly due to a renewed fermentation or a protein instability.

This chapter describes how to degas wine, how to rack from one carboy to another, and how to choose a suitable clarifying agent when needed. Stabilization and filtration are discussed in Chapter NINE and Chapter TWELVE, respectively.

DEGASSING

Wine contains a lot of carbon dioxide (CO_2) gas after fermentation. Until reduced substantially, this gas will impede clarification, even when a clarifying agent is added.

As wine is subjected to various operations, such as racking, stirring in additives and processing aids, and filtering, and given sufficient time, CO_2 gas naturally dissipates on its own. This will occur faster at room temperature than at cooler cellar temperatures.

It's always best to let wine degas naturally, with time and patience, but if you want to accelerate this process, you can degas the wine to remove much of the remaining gas.

First let the wine settle at room temperature for 24 hours, then transfer (*rack*) the wine to a larger carboy or pail to allow for a great amount of foaming. You can degas using the handle of a long mixing spoon and lots of elbow grease, a drill-mounted lees stirrer, or better yet, a vacuum pump or compressor with one of several devices available on the market, such as the Headspace Eliminator and Gas Getter (Figure 8.1).

Degas until there is no more foaming; this should take 5 to 10 minutes to degas a standard carboy when done properly using a vacuum pump and degassing device, or about 20 minutes by manual stirring. Taste the wine as you degas and stop when you no longer detect gas on the palate—there should be no prickly sensation. Don't overdo it as you may then cause the wine to absorb oxygen, which can impact quality. A little gas is good, it adds freshness in whites and rosés, but again, there should be no prickly sensation. The same goes for reds, though you want less gas, so as not to have the acidity of CO_2 reinforce the sensation of tannins.

 Always use a bung with an airlock on a carboy, at least until the wine has released all its fermentation gas. A solid bung (with no airlock) can cause overpressure and the glass carboy to explode before the bung pops out.

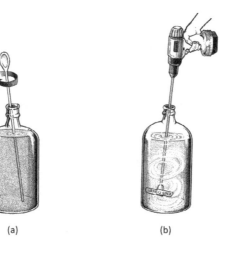

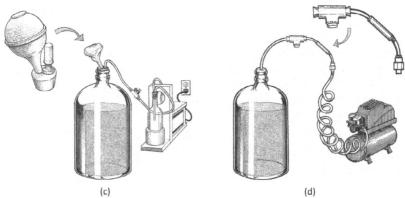

Figure 8.1: Degassing with a) a long mixing spoon, b) a lees stirrer, c) a Headspace Eliminator, and d) Gas Getter

RACKING

From the end of fermentation, right up until bottling, you'll need to rack wine from one carboy to another to separate out wine from the layer of sediment that has formed from natural settling or from the use of a clarifying agent.

You'll be doing several of these rackings depending on the type of wine and how soon you'll want to bottle. If you make one carboy of wine at a time, you can simply rack by gravity, but as you grow your hobby, a diaphragm or vacuum pump will come in handy (Figure 8.2).

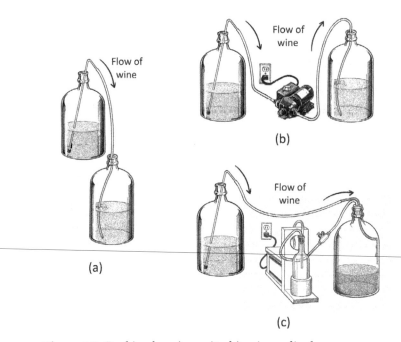

Figure 8.2: Racking by: a) gravity, b) using a diaphragm pump, or c) using a vacuum pump, such as the All In One Wine Pump

To rack by gravity, place the full carboy higher up on a shelf or table and the (empty) receiving carboy on the floor, insert the racking cane with the anti-dregs tip in the carboy and lower the cane about halfway, then suck on the racking hose to start the flow of wine and quickly insert in the receiving carboy. If you prefer not to have to use your mouth to start the flow of wine, you can use an auto-siphon racking cane (see Chapter TWO). Lower the racking cane to just above the sediment layer; don't disturb the sediment and avoid transferring any of it. During racking, slightly tilt and wedge the carboy at an angle to be able to transfer as much wine as possible without losing much. If by mistake you allow that small amount of wine and sediment to mix excessively towards the end of racking, simply transfer the wine to a jug and place an airlock and bung on it, store in the fridge overnight to let the sediment settle again, and then take the wine out and pour carefully into the carboy.

 If you have a starter kit with a pail and carboy only, you'll need to rack twice, first from the carboy to the pail, and then from the pail back into the rinsed carboy.

⚠️ *Racking will cause a lot of foaming in the receiving carboy, especially on the first racking or if using a pump. Use a flow-control clamp on the racking hose or install a dimmer switch on the diaphragm pump to slow down the flow of wine and minimize foaming. Never allow foaming to get past the shoulder of the carboy as a funneling effect will cause foaming and wine to spew out and create a big mess. The amount of foaming decreases with each racking.*

If you want to degas wine while racking, you can place the output hose high in the receiving carboy to splash the wine as it enters the carboy. When you need to minimize oxygen uptake, place the racking hose right at the bottom of the carboy to avoid splashing the wine.

After a racking, you'll have slightly less wine and a small headspace in the carboy. If you don't deal with that headspace, it will slowly cause oxidation and microbial spoilage. The best solution is *topping up*, that is, adding a similar wine or, less ideally, water, to just below the bung. If you add a lot of water, it will dilute and weaken the wine. You might read on the internet that some winemakers drop sanitized marbles into carboys to displace the headspace. That may work well for a very small volume in a jug, but if you need to displace, for example, even a mere ¼ gal (about 1 L) in a carboy, you'll need close to 500 standard-size marbles—that's a lot of marbles! And it will be a pain to get

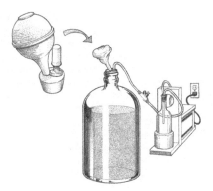

Figure 8.3: All In One Wine Pump and Headspace Eliminator

them out, wash and dry them. It's not worth it. Instead, you can remove the air using a vacuum pump, such as the All In One Wine Pump with a Headspace Eliminator (Figure 8.3). Just be sure to pull a vacuum every couple of weeks to get out any air that might get in.

💡 *If you are using a PET carboy, such as a Better Bottle carboy, and it is just short of a full top-up, simply squeeze the body of the carboy to cause the wine rise up into the neck and then quickly snap a solid-type PET carboy closure into place—you can't use a regular airlock here. The closure forms a perfect seal and keeps the wine from dropping back down.*

You'll want to do as few rackings as needed to minimize oxygen uptake. Racking every 3 months, as many winemakers recommend, is unnecessary. One additional, or perhaps a third, well-executed post-fermentation racking is all you need. From a clarification point-of-view, multiple rackings offer no advantage compared to a single racking done at the end of the same timeframe.

We'll look at specific racking schedules when making wine in Chapters FOURTEEN, FIFTEEN and SIXTEEN. But in general, your first racking will be immediately following completion of fermentation to separate wine as quickly as possible from the gross lees. If allowed to remain in contact with wine for more than two or three days, gross lees could cause hydrogen sulfide (H_2S) and an off-putting rotten-egg smell to develop. A second racking after clarification and stabilization, and a third and final racking just before bottling should suffice. In red winemaking, especially when making rich, bold, tannic reds, you can do more rackings to inject some oxygen to help "soften tannins" if you intend to age just a short period, bottle and drink early.

CLARIFYING ... AND FINING

The term *clarifying* is used to mean to make a wine clear using a clarifying agent that "pulls down" and settles suspended particles. It is often used interchangeably with the word *fining*, although fining is more general, and refers to the use of a fining agent than can modify or remove other substances, such as proteins and tannins, perhaps in addition to clarifying. Here we'll use the term fining for brevity.

Some fining agents may need an additional treatment with a complementary fining agent to work properly or more effectively; this is called *counterfining* or *dual-stage fining*.

Following is a list with descriptions and usage notes of the various fining agents you'll find at your local home winemaking supply store. If you are making vegan wine or if you have any intolerances or allergies, the descriptions will help you make informed decisions on choosing suitable products. There are also many other fining agents of plant origins, such as peas, corn, lentil flour and potatoes, and of yeast origins, but you'll have to research these as they have not become mainstream in home winemaking yet.

Wine still containing a great amount of carbon dioxide (CO_2) gas from fermentation will impede fining speed and efficacy. Either degas the wine or, preferably, give it time to degas naturally before fining.

Bentonite

Bentonite is a type of heavy, soft clay with an extraordinary ability to swell in water, juice or wine, which makes it an excellent fining agent and particularly for treating proteins in whites and rosés. It is usually not recommended in reds as it can strip color. Sodium bentonite has greater binding capacity than calcium bentonite but it creates more sediment, which means a bit more wine loss.

For clarifying or removing proteins, use bentonite at a rate of 1 to 3 tsp per carboy. Most wines will require 2 tsp, but go with 3 tsp when making wine from high-protein or low-tannin vinifera grape varieties, such as Gewürztraminer, Sauvignon Blanc, and Pinot Noir, as well as some hybrids and Native American varieties, such as Concord and Niagara.

To treat a carboy of wine, first slowly add the desired amount of bentonite to hot water, some 50 mL per tsp of bentonite, in a plastic or glass container while constantly stirring vigorously to prevent the clay from clumping. Cap the container tightly and shake vigorously for several minutes, and then shake every so often for about 12 hours or until the next day to completely swell up the clay; you should end up with a very uniform, thick solution with no clumps.

Then, slowly introduce the bentonite solution into the carboy while gently stirring, and continue stirring until thoroughly dispersed. Rack when completely clear. You can expect a significant amount of sediment and some wine loss. If you'll be cold crashing the wine for tartrate stabilization (see the section TARTRATES in Chapter NINE), you can wait and rack just once after the cold treatment—this will help compact the layer of sediment.

Casein

Casein is a type of protein found in milk. It is manufactured into a powder that can be readily dissolved in water, and which is particularly effective for reducing browning and improving color in white wines affected by oxidation. It is also effective for reducing overly bitter tannins in reds. However, it has to be used diligently and carefully as it can strip aromas and color if added excessively.

To treat a carboy, dissolve 1 tbsp in 100 mL of *cold* water and allow to swell for several hours. Introduce very slowly into the carboy while stirring continuously. Allow to settle for a few days to a week, then rack, and if you intend to filter, counterfine with bentonite and rack again before filtering. If you are dealing with a browning problem due to oxidation, counterfine with PVPP (see below) instead of bentonite. You may find a product at your winemaking supply store that combines casein and PVPP into one, which will save you the counterfining treatment.

Chitosan

Chitosan is a polysaccharide derived from chitin, a major structural component of the exoskeleton of crustaceans and insects, as well as in the cell walls of yeasts and filamentous fungi; the latter might be better options if seafood allergies are a concern.

Chitosan is a very effective and rapid-acting fining agent, especially when counterfined with Kieselsol. You'll often find chitosan and Kieselsol packaged together, as in DualFine and Super-Kleer K.C. though the chitosan is derived from shellfish. As there are different chitosan products and usage modes, use as per manufacturer's instructions, but in general, you'll be instructed to first stir in the pack of Kieselsol, wait a few minutes, maybe a day, and then add the pack of chitosan.

Fungi-derived chitosan can be used to treat wines tainted with *Brettanomyces*, a dreaded rogue yeast that can impart an unappealing barnyard smell or other off-aromas (see the section I UNCORKED A BOTTLE AND THE WINE SMELLS LIKE A HORSE'S BEHIND in Chapter SEVENTEEN). It can also be used in wines that have undergone partial malolactic fermentation (MLF), that is, when malic acid has not been completely converted.

Gelatin

Gelatin is a protein derived from animal tissues and bones, and which is recommended for fining aggressive tannins in reds and for compacting loose lees after a bentonite treatment. In whites and rosés, gelatin requires the addition of an equivalent weight of grape tannins to ensure fining efficacy, or a counterfining with Kieselsol to avoid over-fining and possibly making wine unstable with respect to proteins.

As there is a great diversity of gelatin products with varying levels of effectiveness due to different manufacturing methods, follow product instructions for preparing and adding gelatin to wine. Only use unflavored gelatin specifically designed for winemaking, and be careful as there is a risk of over-fining and stripping flavors if not used properly.

To treat a carboy, first soak the instructed amount (it should be around 1 tsp) of gelatin powder in warm water not exceeding 120°F (50°C). Some products may recommend soaking the gelatin in cold water and then heating it to parboil. Add the still-warm gelatin solution to a small volume of wine—about twice the amount of water used—then add to the rest of the wine and stir thoroughly. Let settle until the wine clears completely and then rack.

Isinglass

Isinglass is a protein derived mainly from collagen fibers prepared from the swim bladders of cichlids (tropical spiny-finned freshwater fishes) though traditionally from sturgeons. It is used for clarifying white and rosé wines, particularly oak-aged whites where it enhances aromas without affecting tannins and has minimal impact on color. It strips color to a lesser extent than other protein-type fining agents, such as casein and gelatin.

To treat a carboy, you can add off-the-shelf isinglass liquid directly into wine, or if using isinglass powder, first dissolve ¼ tsp in about 100 mL of *cool* water and allow to swell for 2–3 hours, or as per your product's instructions. Then slowly stir the solution into the carboy. Let settle until the wine clears completely and then rack.

Isinglass tends to throw a fluffier deposit that can to cling to carboy glass making racking a little cumbersome. Either gently stir the wine close to the perimeter of the carboy to dislodge particles, let sediment, then rack, or lightly counterfine with one tsp of hydrated bentonite.

Kieselsol

Kieselsol is made from silicon dioxide (sand), usually as a 30% solution, and which has great fining capacity, both for clarifying and treating proteins, especially when used in combination with gelatin, isinglass, or chitosan as you'll find packaged together under the brand name DualFine, which results in more compact sediment and less wine loss. Kieselsol can be used in any type of wine—white, rosé and red.

To treat a carboy, first add 5–10 mL (1–2 tsp) of 30% kieselsol, or as instructed for your product, directly into the carboy while stirring gently but continuously, then up to 24 hours later, add chitosan or your preferred counterfining agent.

Pectinases

Pectinases (pectic enzymes) are described in the section PECTIN in Chapter NINE.

PVPP

PVPP, short for polyvinylpolypyrrolidone, is a white finely powdered synthetic polymer used to tame excessive bitterness, particularly in red wines that suffer from over-extraction of tannins, and also for fixing browning problems in whites and rosés.

To treat a carboy, first dissolve 2 tbsp of PVPP powder in about 100 mL of water and stir vigorously, let the suspension swell for at least one hour, then introduce into the carboy while stirring continuously until well dispersed. Settling occurs quickly, within hours or several days. If treating white or rosé wine, counterfine with bentonite, and rack immediately after complete settling. A coarse filtration with no. 1 pads or a 10-micron cartridge (see Chapter TWELVE) is recommended after racking.

Sparkolloid

Sparkolloid is a proprietary fining agent; it's a brown-colored alginate powder derived from brown algae. It's very effective in all wines and particularly for treating a stubborn haze. But it tends to produce fairly voluminous lees, therefore, counterfine with a bentonite treatment to compact the less.

To treat a carboy, first boil 100 mL of water in a small saucepan, then stir in 1 (one) tsp of Sparkolloid powder. Let simmer for 20 to 30 minutes while stirring frequently to make sure the powder remains well dissolved and does not form clumps. Slowly introduce the hot Sparkolloid solution into carboy while stirring. Let the wine clear and then rack, or if you want to compact the lees, counterfine with bentonite once the Sparkolloid has settled, let resettle, and rack.

CHAPTER NINE

Stabilizing Wine: Avoiding Faults and Spoilage

*O*nce fermentation is complete, including malolactic fermentation (MLF) if carried out, wine is also treated to protect it against instabilities that could otherwise cause faults or spoilage. This part of the winemaking process is referred to as *stabilization*.

There can be several causes of stability issues: oxidation, renewed alcoholic fermentation due to residual sugar, spontaneous or renewed MLF due to malic acid, wine that won't clear or which has suddenly gone cloudy due to pectin or proteins, and tartrates, a crystalline sediment often found in chilled bottles of white wine. You need to process wine preventively to avoid running into any of these problems. You should also be able to troubleshoot when a problem does occur—it's not always obvious what the cause may be.

This chapter describes how to prevent these instabilities. Chapter SEVENTEEN walks you through the process of troubleshooting, identifying, and resolving these problems.

 You'll often hear of "sterile filtration" as a way to mitigate refermentation problems by filtering out any remaining yeast and bacteria, but this requires equipment and expertise well beyond the means of beginners.

OXIDATION

It is said that oxygen is wine's worst enemy. Well, oxygen is actually desired in red winemaking, but during red-wine aging and in white and rosé winemaking, oxygen can cause wine to prematurely turn a darkish color and slowly lose its delicate aromas and flavors. Oxygen can also cause spoilage by transforming good substances into undesirable ones, for example, alcohol into acetic acid, ethyl acetate, and acetaldehyde. These conditions are generally referred to as *oxidation* and can occur either chemically or under the action of spoilage microbes; for example, acetic acid bacteria thrive in the presence of oxygen and will convert alcohol into acetic acid and volatile acidity (VA) when wine is excessively exposed to oxygen (air) and especially without the protection of a preservative.

To prevent oxidation problems, always top up carboys to within an inch or so of the bung, minimize exposure to air during processing, such as when racking or filtering, and periodically add sulfite as instructed in the section SULFUR DIOXIDE in Chapter FIVE.

You can also use ascorbic acid, also known as vitamin C, in whites and rosés to scavenge oxygen when wine will be exposed to greater amounts of air, for example, when bottling. Ascorbic acid has high antioxidant power, but it must be used in conjunction with sulfite, or else, it can have the opposite effect and cause oxidation. It is not recommended in reds since these contain greater amounts of oxygen that can therefore react with ascorbic acid and cause undesirable results.

To stabilize a carboy of white or rosé with ascorbic acid prior to filtering or bottling, or any other operation that exposes wine to air for long durations, first add sulfite as recommended, then dissolve 1 (one) tsp of ascorbic acid crystals in a little water, introduce into the carboy, and stir thoroughly.

RESIDUAL SUGAR

If you're not fermenting wine completely dry, and that would mean an SG above 0.995, or if you're adding fermentable sugar to sweeten wine (see SWEETENING: BALANCING ACIDITY AND SWEETNESS in Chapter TEN), it can start refermenting anytime when conditions become favorable for yeast to reactivate itself. It can be unsettling, if not dangerous, when fermentation kicks off again in bottles, possibly causing bottles to explode.

To prevent refermentation or as a precaution when unsure, treat the wine with sulfite and sorbate (potassium sorbate). Sorbate is not needed when using commercially produced wine conditioners as these already contain sorbate. If you make natural wine without adding these preservatives, your wine will be at very high risk of refermenting, even if stored at cool cellar temperature.

To stabilize a carboy, add ¼ tsp of KMS (potassium metabisulfite) followed by ½ tsp of sorbate. Dissolve sulfite and sorbate separately and thoroughly in a little *cool* water, stir in the sulfite solution, and then add the sorbate solution *very slowly while stirring continuously*. If you rush the sorbate addition, you risk the possibility of crystals eventually forming in bottles. And don't add more sorbate than instructed here as it can create off aromas and flavors.

Be sure to stabilize at least 2 weeks *before* sweetening, and wait at least 2 weeks after sweetening or before bottling to make sure there is no sedimentation. If there is any sediment, rack before sweetening or bottling. Again, do not rush the sorbate treatment, sweetening, and bottling or you'll likely find tiny white deposits forming in bottles.

 If wine has undergone partial or complete MLF, do not add sorbate as it can give rise to a very unappealing geranium-like smell. Your best bet in this case is to only add sulfite and drink the wine within 6 months, or perhaps add double the amount of sulfite if you want to age the wine longer.

 Sorbate does not protect wine on its own; it must be used with sulfite.

 Sorbate inhibits renewed fermentation by keeping yeast in check; it does not inhibit or kill active yeast, and therefore, it cannot be used to—and will not—stop an active fermentation.

RESIDUAL MALIC ACID

Wine contains naturally occurring malic acid, which, in reds, is most often converted into lactic acid by malolactic fermentation (MLF). If you are not protecting wine with any preservatives, or if MLF was only partial so that there is residual malic acid, malolactic bacteria can jump back into action and restart metabolizing malic acid into lactic acid when conditions become favorable.

To prevent renewed malolactic activity or as a precaution when unsure, treat the wine with sulfite and lysozyme, or, alternatively, with chitosan.

To stabilize a carboy of wine, add ¼ tsp KMS and 2 tsp of lysozyme powder. First dissolve the sulfite powder in a little water and add to the carboy. Rehydrate the lysozyme powder in 50 mL of *warm* water, stir gently for one minute, and allow to soak for at least 45 minutes, stirring periodically during soaking. Slowly stir the lysozyme suspension into the carboy, let the wine stand for a minimum of 1 (one) week, preferably two, and then rack carefully.

If you are adding lysozyme to white wine, counterfine with bentonite. Lysozyme is a protein and can cause a protein instability. This is not an issue in reds as tannins will aggregate with and remove proteins.

As there are different chitosan products and usage modes, use as per manufacturer's instructions.

PECTIN

Pectin is a viscous, structural polysaccharide found in the cell walls of all plant tissues; it acts as the "cement" between cellulose fibers. Pectin in grapes is found predominantly in the skins and therefore it occurs in higher amounts in reds owing to greater extraction into juice during maceration.

Pectin is usually not an issue in wines made from European grape varieties (viniferas) as it is almost completely broken down during fermentation by naturally occurring pectin-type enzymes, called pectic enzymes or pectinases. But non-vinifera varieties, particularly *V. labrusca* and notably Concord, as well as many fruit wines, especially citrus fruit, can have very high levels that can leave excessive residual pectin and cause clarification and filtration problems if not treated sufficiently. As a precaution, treat any juice from viniferas and non-vinifera varieties that will be macerated with skins.

There are many, many types of pectic enzyme products in powder or liquid form, each with different uses. Different products are also available whether using pectic enzymes at the juice stage, or at the wine stage to address a pectin problem—more is needed in wine as pectic enzymes are less effective in alcohol. In general, you'll need about 2 tsp of pectic enzyme powder per carboy of juice or for up to 100 lbs (45 kg) of crushed grapes, but follow your product's instructions. Dissolve the powder in *cold* water, never warm or hot because heat deactivates the enzymes.

PROTEINS

Proteins are very large, naturally occurring molecules formed by amino acids, which can still be present in significant amounts in white and rosé wine following fermentation. Wine may appear perfectly clear, but proteins can break down, more so with increasing temperature, causing a haze and possibly forming white specks or sediment. Wine must be treated with enzymes capable of breaking down these proteins before they cause a problem—these enzymes are known as proteases. Since high temperature is the main factor in protein stability, it is also referred to as heat stability.

Proteins are generally not an issue in reds because these bind to and precipitate with tannins. Proteases can be added as a preventive when making wine using high-protein or low-tannin grape varieties, such as Gewürztraminer, Sauvignon Blanc, and Pinot Noir, as well as some hybrids and Native American varieties, such as Concord and Niagara. In whites, and particularly in fruity, early-drinking styles of wines where there are negligible amounts of tannins, proteins must be removed using a suitable fining agent; bentonite is the most common one—use as instructed in the section the CLARIFYING … AND FINING in Chapter EIGHT.

TARTRATES

If you have ever forgotten a bottle of white wine at the back of the fridge, you may have discovered crystals formed at the bottom. It can be unsettling as the crystals look like tiny shards of broken glass. What you really witnessed are tartrate crystals, what many call "wine diamonds." They form from tartaric acid and potassium when wine is held cold sufficiently long. Tartrates are totally harmless, and in fact, tartrates from the wine industry are a major source in the production of cream of tartar used in baking. Not all winemakers will agree that tartrates are acceptable. Those that think they are not, will process wine to ensure it is protected against tartrates forming in bottles.

Wine can be made stable against tartrates by one of two methods: by chilling, often referred to as cold crashing, or, if that is not an option, by adding a stabilizer that inhibits tartrate formation.

Whites and rosés are always stabilized against tartrates as these wines are typically chilled prior to serving. Reds don't need to be stabilized against tartrates if served at warmer temperatures or if they will never be stored cooler than the temperature of your cellar or storage area.

To stabilize a batch of wine against tartrates using the chilling method, transfer the carboy to your fridge (never in the freezer) and let stand for at least 2 weeks at the coldest temperature you can manage, or at typical refrigerator temperature, around 40°F (4°C). Then take the carboy out and see if tartrates have formed; if you see crystals at the bottom, let the wine warm up to cellar or room temperature, then rack carefully into another carboy. If you notice crystals stuck to the glass, use a stirring device and stir the wine close to the perimeter of the carboy to dislodge the crystals. Allow the crystals to fall to the bottom and then rack to another carboy. If no tartrates have formed, that means your wine is already stable and you need take no further action. As a precaution, wait another week or two before bottling to make sure no more tartrates form as these can take time to form. Note that, if you give a bottle to a friend who stores it in a fridge at a colder temperature than yours, you can expect a call alerting you of tartrates in your wine.

Keep in mind that chilling wine results in a drop in acidity and a change in pH if you see tartrates. It's hard to predict those changes; simply re-measure acidity (TA) and pH to determine actual changes. Cold crashing is also a good strategy in cases where you need to drop acidity in an effort to achieve better balance. Refer to the sidebar on TARTARIC ACID AND TARTRATES in the section ACIDITY AND pH in Chapter FIVE on p. 77 for more information on acidity and pH related to tartrates.

 Never place a glass carboy outdoors for chilling at freezing temperatures—it can cause the glass to crack and the carboy to break, and possibly cause serious injury. If you want to take advantage of a cold spell, transfer the wine to a PET carboy, which resists cold temperatures; just don't let the wine freeze. Dry wine starts freezing at about 20°F (–6°C).

If you blend wines, always blend before chilling; blending wines after chilling does not guarantee a stable blend.

If chilling is not an option, you can add a tartrate inhibitor. You'll likely find metatartaric acid (in powder form) at most stores, but it's not recommended, at least not for wines you intend to age for 6 months or more, as its efficacy is short-lived. The best inhibitors might not be available in home winemaking supply stores, but you may be able to find them online, albeit, likely in large formats for treating large volumes. If you can find a product that contains carboxymethyl cellulose (CMC), it works really well in whites and rosés; it may impact color and mouthfeel in reds. For reds, and for all wines, potassium polyaspartate is a more effective inhibitor with no impact on color and mouthfeel. Follow your product's instructions for the recommended dosage. Typically, you'll need about 25 mL per carboy when either carboxymethyl cellulose or potassium polyaspartate are prepared as liquid solutions. Since these inhibitors do not drop tartrates, like cold stabilization does, these cause no change in tartaric acid levels, and therefore acidity (TA) and pH are unaffected.

Always cold crash or add an inhibitor before filtering and bottling, so as not to alter the wine's stability. For the same reason, don't make any acid adjustments by adding tartaric acid after tartrate stabilization.

CHAPTER TEN

Sweetening: Balancing Acidity and Sweetness

*I*f you are partial to sweeter-style wines, or if you have a slightly acidic wine that is just a tad too sour for your taste and you don't want to deacidify, you can simply add sugar or other sweetening agent to suit your palate and to achieve better balance. This is practice is commonly referred to as *backsweetening* in home winemaking, but we'll simply refer to it as *sweetening* here.

Sweetening is different from chaptalization. Sweetening implies the addition of a sweetening agent to a finished wine, whereas chaptalization refers to the addition of fermentable sugars to juice to raise Potential Alcohol (PA) (see the subsection *Chaptalization* in the section SPECIFIC GRAVITY AND POTENTIAL ALCOHOL in Chapter FIVE on p. 71).

Generally, it's always best to ferment a wine completely dry, i.e., SG at or below 0.995, and then sweeten, unless you prefer a sweeter-style wine with lower alcohol, in which case you would need to stop fermentation before it runs dry (see the subsection *Stopping an Active Fermentation* in the section CONDUCTING AND MONITORING FERMENTATION in Chapter SIX on p. 104).

There are many options for sweetening wine: you can add sucrose, glucose or fructose; use a wine conditioner; use reserved press-run grape juice or grape-juice concentrate in cans or from a kit; add glycerin; add honey, or brown or caramelized sugar; or, add stevia or an artificial sweetener, such sucralose or xylitol.

If you add any sweetener consisting of *fermentable* sugars, basically all of the above except stevia, artificial sweeteners, and glycerin, you'll need to treat the wine with sorbate and sulfite *before* sweetening to prevent a renewed fermentation in bottles. Wine conditioners already contain sorbate. The section RESIDUAL SUGAR in Chapter NINE describes the process of treating wine with sorbate and sulfite.

> *Never use sorbate in wine that has undergone malolactic fermentation (MLF); malolactic bacteria can metabolize sorbate and give rise to an off-putting geranium odor.*

To avoid disappointments, always conduct bench trials to determine the amount of sweetening agent needed to hit your sweet spot. Be careful with stevia and artificial sweeteners as these may not necessarily complement grape wines, but you can certainly experiment with those if wanting to create a different style.

Sucrose, which is table sugar, is readily available and the easiest to add; we'll use it here to illustrate how to sweeten wine, and this is best done by using a 10% sugar solution.

Heat about 75 mL of water and transfer to a small heat-resistant beaker or cup and dissolve *exactly* 10 g of sugar. If you can't weigh the sugar, use two flush teaspoons, although this will give you a slightly higher concentration than 10%, but that's okay. Then add a pinch of acid, either tartaric acid or citric acid; this is to break down the sucrose. Stir well until all is perfectly dissolved. Let cool down to room temperature, then transfer the syrupy solution to a 100-mL graduated cylinder. Rinse the beaker or cup with a little tap water and transfer to the cylinder, and add water as needed to bring the volume to exactly 100 mL.

You'll run bench trials using 50-mL wine samples, and 0.5 mL of 10% sugar solution in 50 mL of wine adds approximately 1 g/L or 0.1% of sugar. If you then want to trial, for example, adding 10 g/L of sugar, you'll need to add 5.0 mL of 10% sugar solution to a 50-mL wine sample. One-, 5- and 10-mL syringes will come in handy here. Be sure to stir samples when sweetening.

Get as many wine tasting glasses as samples you want to trial. You'll also need a control sample, that is, with no sugar addition, which you'll need to compare to the sweetened samples.

If you are not sure of your desired sweetness, pick a fairly large range of sugar additions to run your trials; for example, conduct bench trials by adding 10 g/L, 20 g/L and 30 g/L of sugar, and if you find that 20 g/L is not enough but that 30 g/L is too sweet, then you can perform a second round of trials with a narrower range.

Once you have determined the right dosage for your taste and desired style, simply scale up the dosage to your batch, and add the sugar to the wine. For example, if you have determined that you best prefer the sample with 10 g/L of added sugar, then you'll need to add 190 g (6.7 oz) to a 5-gal (19-L) batch. Remember that, if using sucrose, you need to dissolve the sugar in heated water with a little acid, letting that cool down before adding to wine. You'll need to remove just a little bit of wine from the carboy to make room for the amount of 10% solution to add, then top up as needed with the wine, and if you have any left over, save it for topping up another carboy or drink it up.

 Home winemakers often work with target SG numbers and use some conversion factor or table to determine the amount of sugar to add to hit that SG. This doesn't work given the complexity of wine and estimating sugars, especially at low SG. Adding the "right" amount of sugar to a desired sweetness can only be performed by conducting tasting bench trials as described above.

You can download the SWEETENING BENCH TRIALS tool at ModernHomeWinemaking.com; it will walk you through the process of conducting trials to determine how much table sugar to add to sweeten wine to your desired taste.

CHAPTER ELEVEN

Why, When and How to Blend Wines

You'll often want—or need—to blend two or more wines to remedy a deficiency, to maintain a consistent style that you like, or to create a different style altogether.

To be clear, a deficiency is not a fault, but rather, a shortcoming. Perhaps you have a weak, low-ABV wine in need of some extra oomph, and that high-ABV wine you made last season might just do the trick to create a better balanced wine. Or maybe you have an under-extracted red that needs a tannin boost to give it greater structure, more mouthfeel, and you have a full-bodied red sitting around waiting for a blending partner.

However! Never blend a problem wine, a spoiled wine, with a perfectly sound one, at least not if you can help it. You'll only end up with a disappointing, subpar wine. If you have a bad batch with high volatile acidity (VA), ethyl acetate, acetaldehyde or some advanced oxidation problem, accept the situation, learn from it and discard the wine. It's a tough one to swallow, pun intended. But why would you want to blend? You'll only be infecting and ruining another batch of good wine. And you would need a lot of good wine to fix a bad one.

Blending is, however, a great tool for making the same style of wine year after year, or for creating different styles of wines, wines that are greater than the sum of the parts, as the saying goes. The idea is to bring together complementary wines to take advantage of the characteristics of each varietal, without any aroma, flavor or other characteristic dominating, maintaining that all-important balance we learned about in Chapter ONE.

There are countless examples of well-known traditional blends. In reds, Cabernet Sauvignon and Merlot go hand in hand, and so do Grenache, Syrah, and Mourvèdre. In whites, Riesling and Gewürztraminer, and Sémillon with Sauvignon Blanc are perfect matches. The possibilities are endless, especially in home winemaking where there are no rules as in commercial winemaking. Try different combinations, traditional and new ones, and in different percentages. And why not blend wines made from European varieties with Native American varieties or hybrids. Try blending Baco Noir, Chambourcin and Maréchal Foch in any combination, then try adding some Cabernet, either Sauvignon or Franc.

You can also blend wines produced from grapes from different grape-growing regions or even vintages, from different carboys or your best lots, or even the same wine fermented separately with different yeast strains. It's also perfectly okay with no one raising an eyebrow to blend a smidgen of richly colored red wine into a white to create a vibrant rosé for summer sipping.

And yes! You can blend wines made from grapes and other fruits to craft myriad styles as many amateurs do: blackberry wine with a Cabernet or Merlot, apple wine with a Riesling, and peach wine with a rosé from Grenache. Each of these fruit wines enhances those same subtle fruit aromas and flavors found in the grape wines.

The challenge with blending, and especially if you are just starting out making wine, is having wines to blend. So if you want to experiment with blending and create different, exciting styles, start making wines from various varieties you can source, perhaps make one or two batches from your favorite varieties and then make two or three others from new (to you) varieties.

There are also logistical issues depending on what wines and volumes you have available as well as your processing capacity that you'll all need to assess. If you have only a couple of small batches, you may have no choice but to blend them completely. And then you'll need a larger vessel to hold the blended wine. If you don't have an appropriately sized demijohn (a larger glass vessel), you can blend into a large vat and then rack back into carboys, but do so as gently as possible to minimize oxygen pickup, which could otherwise cause wine to age a little faster.

Okay! So how to go about blending now?

First, set your objectives. Are you wanting to blend to create a specific style or to fix a deficiency? For example, if you need to boost % ABV by even 2% ABV, know that you may need a significant amount of a blending wine, which might change the style of each wine. Research and understand each varietal to know what characteristics each will bring to the blend.

Second, run bench trials, extensive bench trials with lots of glasses, with as many combinations as possible. Make it fun! Invite a couple of friends or family members, those who will be drinking your wine and whose palates you trust, to help with the process. Just don't let it turn into a party; maintain focus. And be sure the wines to be blended are tasted at typical serving temperature. That means, pre-chill whites and rosés and bring the reds out of your cool cellar ahead of the trials.

Once you've determined that perfect blend and in the desired proportions, *blend into a single batch* for homogeneity; this is important. Blend the wines and set aside for several weeks, then taste again to make sure that it smells and tastes as the day you created the blend. Allow time to make any further adjustments as needed. Don't be in a rush to bottle.

A word of caution!

Blending stable wines does not guarantee a stable blend. Really? Yes. For example, if two whites are cold stable, one with high tartaric acid and low potassium and the other with low tartaric acid and high potassium, the now high-tartaric, high-potassium blend will need to be cold stabilized to make sure it does not drop tartrates in bottles later on. Likewise, don't blend a wine that has undergone malolactic fermentation (MLF) with one that hasn't. Avoid blending a malolactic-fermented grape wine with a fruit wine that has residual sugar and which was stabilized with sorbate (see the section RESIDUAL SUGAR in Chapter NINE).

To blend wines to get to a desired % ABV or acidity (TA) using two wines of known % ABV or TA, use the Pearson Square (see the section AMELIORATION in Chapter FIVE) to determine the proportion of each wine.

Remember that the Pearson Square only works for linear relationships, so it cannot be used for pH since it's a logarithmic function. You'll have to go by trial-and-error by blending the two wines in various combinations until you hit your desired pH.

Let's work through an example.

EXAMPLE

Pearson Square – blending two wines to increase TA

You have a 5-gal (19-L) batch of low-acid Chambourcin wine with a TA of 5.2 g/L (this is the B value) that you would like to increase to 6.0 g/L (this is the C value) using Frontenac wine with a TA of 10.0 g/L (this is the A value). Determine as follows how much Frontenac you need to add to the Chambourcin to achieve the desired TA:

10.0	0.8
6.0	
5.2	4.0

The Pearson Square says that you need 0.8 parts of Frontenac wine for 4.0 parts of Chambourcin wine, or:

$$Volume \ of \ Frontenac \ needed \ (gal) = 5 \ gal \times \frac{0.8}{4.0} = 1.0 \ gal$$

This example illustrates that, even for what may seem like a small adjustment in TA from 5.2 to 6.0 g/L, blending to make such corrections may require significant amounts of the second wine (20% here), which could substantially alter the character of the original wine.

The Pearson Square is easy to use but you can only work with two wines at a time, which makes it tedious and complicated when blending several wines. You can download BLENDING CALCULATORS at ModernHome Winemaking.com; these will walk you through the calculations, and also help you figure out the final % ABV, TA and percent of each wine in the blend.

CHAPTER TWELVE

Should I Filter My Wines?

There is probably no winemaking topic more controversial than that of filtration. Many opine that it is not needed (and similarly for fining), that filtration strips wine of color, aromas and flavors, that it changes the character of the wine, and that natural sedimentation and time are sufficient to obtain a clear wine.

If you prefer not to filter and you tolerate some sediment, or if you drink your wines relatively young, then sure, you can forego filtration. But if you want that extra sparkle and brilliance, or if you'll be submitting wines into competitions or gifting bottles to friends and family, then filtration is the way to go.

What about color, aromas, flavors, and wine character?

Regarding color, what you're filtering is what will either stick to bottle glass or eventually sediment. If you reuse bottles, then you'll have to clean those with a special cleaner, such as percarbonate, as a simple water rinse often won't remove stubborn color stains from glass. Also, sediment in bottles is okay in reds, if not excessive, but much less tolerated in whites and rosés. As for aromas, flavors and character, filter pads and cartridges used in winemaking cannot filter such tiny molecules as to affect aromas and flavors. What is actually happening is that wine picks up a little oxygen that causes a temporary, transient change in smell and taste. It can take days, perhaps weeks, many weeks, depending on the wine, for it to return to what it was like before filtering. It's the same with bottling. And if filter pads are not prepared properly or if filtration is poorly executed as to allow excessive oxygen to become absorbed, yes, those will irreversibly and negatively alter wine quality.

This chapter describes how to filter wine properly with no impact on quality.

 You'll often hear of "sterile filtration" as a way to mitigate refermentation problems by filtering out any remaining yeast and bacteria, but this requires equipment and expertise well beyond the means of beginners.

FILTRATION EQUIPMENT

Figure 12.1 illustrates some of the more common home winemaking filtration equipment.

(a)   (b)

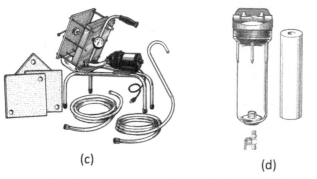

(c)   (d)

Figure 12.1: Filtration equipment: a) round plate-and-frame filter and pads; b) Buon Vino Mini Jet and filter pads; c) Buon Vino Super Jet and filter pads; and d) 10-inch filter housing and cartridge.

Filtration for small-scale home winemaking makes use of single-use, disposable filter media, namely, pads and cartridges, which filter to different extents based on their porosity. Filter medium porosity is expressed in microns and ranges from 10 microns down to 0.45 micron, and the larger the micron number, the more porous the filter medium. Filter media in the 5 to 10 microns range are used for coarse filtering, 2 to 5 microns for polishing filtering, and 0.45 to 1 micron for fine filtering. The idea is that, to avoid pulling your hair out due to clogging of the pads and exposing wine excessively to oxygen, you should always step-filter. That is, filter successively down using first a coarse filter followed by a polishing filter, and lastly, a fine filter.

Filter pads for home winemaking often use a simple designation instead of microns. Round filter pads are identified as AF1, AF2, AF3, AF4, and AF5 corresponding to micron sizes 8, 4.5, 2.5, 0.8, and 0.5, respectively, while Buon Vino filter pads are identified as no. 1, no. 2, and no. 3 corresponding to micron size 5, 1.8, and 0.5. Table 12.1 lists common types of filtration and filter media available for small batches.

Table 12.1: Types of filtration and filter media available for filtering small batches.

Type of filtration	Approximate microns range	Round pads	Buon Vino pads[1]
Coarse	5–10	AF1, AF2	No. 1
Polishing	2–5	AF3	No. 2
Fine	0.5–1	AF4, AF5	No. 3

[1]Buon Vino Mini Jet and Super Jet filters use different-sized pads.

In any filtration setup, wine is "pushed" or "pulled" through the filter medium using a small diaphragm or vacuum pump. Diaphragm pump-powered filtration systems filter by moving wine from one carboy or pail, through the pump and filter medium, and into another carboy or pail. Vacuum-type filtration systems filter by pulling wine from a carboy or pail, then through the filter medium, and into another carboy—the wine never flows through the vacuum pump. The advantage of a vacuum-type system is that the wine is protected from air in the receiving carboy. You cannot vacuum filter into a second pail as a vacuum would cause the pail to implode.

The round plate-and-frame filter is most economical for filtering a single carboy if you already have a small pump; otherwise, go for an integrated filter system, such as Buon Vino's Mini Jet. For larger or more batches to be filtered the same day, your best bet is either Buon Vino's Super Jet or to use a housing with a disposable polypropylene-spun microfiber cartridge and a diaphragm or vacuum pump, such as the All In One Wine Pump. 10-inch housings and cartridges are the most common; you'll find them at any good store that sells water filtration components.

FILTERING WITH FILTER PADS

Figure 12.2 illustrates two typical filtration setups using filter pads: a) round plate-and-frame filter, and b) Buon Vino Super Jet.

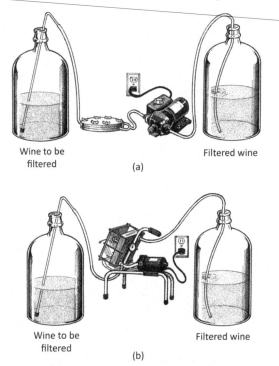

Wine to be filtered

Filtered wine

(a)

Wine to be filtered

Filtered wine

(b)

Figure 12.2: Typical filtration setups: a) round plate-and-frame filter, and b) Buon Vino Super Jet

There are three very important points to remember when setting up a filtration system that uses disposable filter pads:

1. Filter pads have a smooth side and a rough side; these must be positioned correctly between filtration plates as per the system's instructions so that wine flows in from the rough side and out the smooth side. Be sure you understand the configuration and setup of your system.

   In the Buon Vino Mini Jet, pads are inserted between plates with the rough side of all pads pointing away from the back plate; in the Buon Vino Super Jet, all pads are inserted between plates with the rough side pointing towards the pump. Be sure that the holes in pads all line up perfectly with the holes in the plates. Each of these setups uses three filter pads.

2. If you intend to step-filter, you'll need to do successive filter runs; do *not* use a mix of pads with different ratings.

3. Condition the pads to avoid imparting a cardboard taste to wine.

To condition pads, first prepare about 3 gallons (12 L) of sulfite–citric solution in a small bucket. Refer to the section SANITIZING in Chapter THREE for instructions on preparing a sulfite–citric solution.

 Never use alkaline (caustic) products or products containing detergents or foaming agents for cleaning or sanitizing filter pads as these can leave residues that can negatively affect the taste or appearance of wine.

Soak the set of pads in clean, fresh water until completely saturated, until there is no more bubbling. Take each pad out and let drip briefly, then insert each one at a time in the frame as per your system's instructions, and tighten all bolts by hand as hard as you can. If you prefer to insert the pads dry, only loosely tighten all bolts, run water through the filter system and allow the pads to swell up completely (this will cause quite a bit of leakage), and only then completely tighten all bolts until leakage stops.

Install the racking cane with its anti-dregs tip and hoses. Insert both the racking cane and out hose in the bucket with sulfite–citric solution, turn on the pump, and let the solution recirculate for about 10 minutes to sanitize the whole system—pump, filter plates, filter pads and hoses. When done, slightly raise the racking cane just above the sulfite–citric solution and let run for just a few seconds to empty the filter system of any leftover solution.

Transfer the racking cane to a pail filled with about 5 gal (or about 20 L) of clean, fresh water, and place the out tube into another pail or carboy where you'll collect flushed water for possible reuse. Start the pump to rinse the entire system and flush out any leftover sulfite–citric solution. While flushing, taste the water regularly; you can stop the rinsing when the water has no cardboard taste. When done, slightly raise the racking cane just above the water level and let run for just a few seconds to empty the filter system of any leftover water.

You are now ready to filter wine.

At this point, the filter pads still contain some water, and therefore, when you start the filtration run, you'll get some water at first; you'll need to decide when water becomes wine and start collecting wine in the receiving carboy.

Insert the racking cane in the carboy (or pail) with previously racked wine to be filtered. Hold the output hose over the floor drain or a small container. Start the pump and watch for the water at the output hose. As soon as the water turns to wine, judging from the color, place the out hose in the receiving carboy and let filtration run its course.

If your system is equipped with a pressure gauge, monitor filtration pressure to make sure it stays within the manufacturer's prescribed maximum; if not, just make sure that wine flows at a good, consistent rate. If pads clog up, you may not be able to complete the filtration run, and you'll need to start over with a coarser grade of pads. It's a time-wasting pain, so plan carefully.

Plate-and-frame filter systems will leak—just a little—during filtration; this is normal. If there is excessive leakage, try tightening the plates; if it persists, you're likely trying to filter with pads of too low a rating or the wine is not filter-ready, that is, it has not been clarified sufficiently.

Once the pump is working and wine is being filtered, avoid turning the pump off/on as it can affect filter efficiency and clarity of the wine.

When done, dispose of the pads—they can be composted—and flush the pump and hoses with clean water (or the water you had saved from the sanitizing step). Clean the pump by running and recirculating a mild solution of carbonate or percarbonate cleaner (see the section SANITIZING in Chapter THREE). Immerse in a similar solution all hoses and parts that have come into contact with wine. Rinse the pump, hoses, and parts with fresh, clean water, let dry and store away.

FILTERING WITH CARTRIDGES

You can use disposable cartridges right out of the *unopened* package without sanitizing if they have been stored properly; however, it's always best to clean and sanitize cartridges to reduce spoilage risks from possible contaminants left over from manufacturing.

To filter efficiently, wine must be filtered across the whole length of a cartridge, and this means that *the filter housing should always be full during filtration*. All too often those inexperienced with cartridge filtration will have wine only partially fill the housing and leave a good portion of the cartridge not filtering. This happens when the filter housing sits above the level of the wine (to be filtered) or has not been primed properly. Some filter housings, such as Tenco's Tandem used with the Enolmatic bottler, are equipped with a bypass/purge valve to purge air out of the housing and equilibrate pressure. You can easily install a bypass/purge valve on your housing if not so equipped already.

In the following procedure, you can use a filtration configuration with a filter housing and medium using a diaphragm or vacuum pump (Figure 12.3).

 Make sure that the carboy of wine to be filtered is ABOVE the filter housing so that the filter housing fills up completely and filtering uses the entire length of the cartridge. This means having the bottom of the carboy always above the highest point of the housing, as shown in Figure 12.3.

Tightly secure all hose connections with hose clamps, keeping in mind that dry wine, that is wine with SG less than 1.000, is less dense than water, and therefore, you might still get a leak once you start filtering wine even though there was no leak during sanitizing and rinsing.

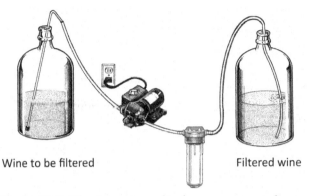

Wine to be filtered   Filtered wine

Figure 12.3: Filtering using a diaphragm pump and cartridge; note that the wine level is above the housings

To sanitize a new cartridge, first prepare some 3 gal (12 L) of sulfite–citric solution in a bucket (see the section on SANITIZING in Chapter THREE). Note that since you have to sanitize the filter housing, you'll be sanitizing the cartridge too even if it is not required. With the bucket of solution sitting above the filter housing, insert the racking cane and out hose in the sulfite–citric solution, turn on the pump, and allow the housing to fill up completely, then let the solution recirculate for about 10 minutes. When done, slightly raise the racking cane just above the sulfite–citric solution and let run for just a few seconds to empty the filter system of any leftover solution.

Transfer the racking cane to a pail filled with about 5 gal (or about 20 L) of clean, fresh water, and the output tube into another pail or carboy. Start the pump and let the housing fill up completely, then rinse the entire system. Collect the outflow of water for possible reuse. When done, slightly raise the racking cane just above the water and let run for just a few seconds to empty the filter system of any leftover water. If there is any water left in the housing, unscrew the housing, drain and replace, or simply drain via the bottom drain valve, if so equipped.

You are now ready to filter wine.

At this point, the cartridge may still contain a significant amount of water, and therefore, when you start the filtration run, you'll get some water at first; you'll need to decide when water becomes wine and start collecting wine in the receiving carboy.

Insert the racking cane in the carboy (or pail) with previously racked wine to be filtered. Hold the output hose over the floor drain or a small container. Start the pump and allow the housing to fill up completely, and watch for the water at the output hose. As soon as the water turns to wine, judging from the color, place the output hose in the receiving carboy and let filtration run its course.

If your system is equipped with a pressure gauge, monitor filtration pressure to make sure it stays within the manufacturer's prescribed maximum; if not, just make sure that wine flows at a good, consistent rate and that the *housing remains full to the top until the end of the run.* If the cartridge clogs up, you may not be able to complete the filtration run, and you'll need to start over with a coarser grade cartridge.

Dispose of the cartridge and flush the pump, hoses and housing with clean water (or the water you had saved from the sanitizing step). Clean hoses and housing by running and recirculating a mild solution of carbonate or percarbonate cleaner. And lastly, rinse hoses and housing with fresh, clean water, let dry and store away.

CHAPTER THIRTEEN

Making Bottling Fun

Bottling may seem like a simple task—prepare bottles, fill them up, cork, and, optionally, dress each with a capsule and label. A lot of planning actually goes into bottling, from making sure the wine is bottle-ready, to choosing and sourcing bottles, corks, and capsules, to designing and printing your own labels. All too often, home winemakers, and especially novices, rush to bottle only to wonder why corks are popping out, why sediment is forming, or why is the wine not tasting like it did on the day it was bottled.

First, make sure that the wine is bottle-ready. That means, it has been adequately clarified and stabilized, as well as aged so that it tastes to your liking. If you are blending two or more wines, give the blend some time "to come together," then taste it again after a few weeks or months and decide if it is bottle-ready. See Chapter ELEVEN for more information on blending.

So! Plan well ahead, source or order all your bottling needs, and only bottle when ready.

BOTTLES, CORKS, CAPSULES, AND LABELS

You need 25 standard 750-mL bottles for a 5-gal (19-L) carboy of wine, plus 25 each of corks, capsules, and labels.

Bottles

750-mL bottles with a cork finish are the easiest to source and to apply a cork to, but you can use 375-mL bottles or whatever other size you can find and that you prefer. Screw cap-type bottles require special, expensive equipment to apply the screw cap. You can reuse bottles and hand-tighten screw caps if you don't intend to age the wine for more than several months. That's because the liner under the screw cap no longer provides a perfect seal once used.

Any bottle shape (Figure 13.1) that you fancy will do, depending on how you'll store bottles. High-shouldered Bordeaux-style bottles stack nicely, Burgundy bottles less so, while tall sloping-shouldered Alsace or Hoch-style bottles don't stack very well.

Figure 13.1: Most common wine bottle shapes: a) Bordeaux; b) Burgundy; and c) Alsace or Hoch

Any glass color will do so as long as you don't expose wine to strong sources of light, which could otherwise cause wine to oxidize. You may want to use clear-glass (known as flint) bottles for whites, rosés and fruit wines to showcase their color, and use green- or brown-colored bottles for reds as these all look dark in flint bottles in any case. The darker color provides more protection in case wine is exposed to light.

If you are reusing bottles, be sure to wash them thoroughly *before* storing them away to avoid mold. Then wash again and sanitize when ready to bottle wine.

Corks

The standard closure for 750-mL bottles (as well as 375- and 1.5-L bottles) is what is referred to as a size no. 9 "cork" although it can be made not only from natural cork material but also synthetic polymers.

 The more general and correct terms for bottle closures are "stoppers" or "closures" as they do not imply any material as "corks" does; however, here, we'll adopt the latter as it is commonly used to refer to any type of closure, for example, "synthetic cork," used in standard, non-screw cap bottles.

Corks come in various quality levels, and you really get what you pay for here. Most will work just fine if you don't intend to age wine for more than 12 to 18 months, but you'll need better quality corks the longer you expect to age wine.

The best cork-type stoppers (Figure 13.2) are: natural corks, which are punched out as single pieces from the outermost layer of the bark of Cork Oak; and micro-agglomerate corks, manufactured from very finely ground cork granules glued together with a binding agent and which provide a more uniform structure with a much denser and stronger body. Agglomerated corks use coarser granules of lesser quality. So-called 1+1 or twin-disc corks have an agglomerated body but with a natural-cork disc at each end. Colmated corks, manufactured

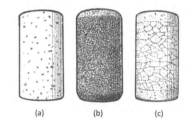

Figure 13.2: Cork-type stoppers: a) natural; b) micro-agglomerated; and c) agglomerated

from lower-quality parts of the cork bark and which have had cork dust applied with an adhesive to fix defects and imperfections, also work well for wine intended to be consumed within a year.

Synthetic corks are manufactured entirely from polymers, such as low-density polyethylene (LDPE), or from plant-based biopolymers, such as sugar cane. Unlike the rock-hard synthetic corks of yesteryear, these are now much easier to insert and to uncork too. Just beware that not all synthetic corks work well with manual corkers. Some corks are very hard to compress; a floor corker is recommended.

No. 9 refers to the size (diameter) of corks and comes in a standard length of 1½ inches. The smaller no. 8 stoppers are easier to insert but don't provide as tight a seal; these may cause leakage and, more importantly, allow too much oxygen into bottles and cause wine to oxidize and age prematurely.

Only buy as many corks as you'll need on bottling day. Most suppliers sell packs of 30 corks for bottling a 5- or 6-gal (19- or 23-L) batch of wine or in packs of 100. Reseal unused corks in a Ziploc bag and remove as much air as possible, and use them as soon as possible, within 3 to 6 months. There is no need to soak corks in water or to sanitize when used fresh out from a new, unopened bag.

If the bag had been previously opened and you need to sanitize the corks, you can build a simple "sulfite humidor." You need to do this several days in advance of bottling.

Pour a small amount of sulfite–citric solution (see the section SANITIZING in Chapter THREE) in a pail. Place the required number of corks in a sanitized lightweight plastic bowl, seat it on the surface of the solution, and close the pail tight with its lid. Let stand for several days in an area at room temperature to allow humidity in the pail to rise and to allow sulfur dioxide (SO_2) gas to sanitize the corks without soaking.

Capsules

Capsules add a nice finish to bottles. PVC heat-shrink capsules (Figure 13.3a) are the most common and are very easy and quick to apply. Just slide capsules on bottles and then apply heat using a heat gun, the kind for stripping paint, or by using steam over a kettle of boiling water (Figure 13.3b).

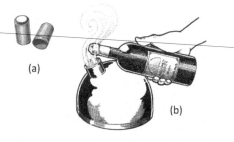

(a)

(b)

Figure 13.3: a) PVC heat-shrink capsules and b) shrinking a capsule

Labels

You have many options for labels: buy generic off-the-shelf, ready-to-apply labels; download predesigned labels, then print; submit your artwork to a label company who will create and print custom labels; or do it all and design, personalize and print your own using your favorite art or photo-editing app.

If you'll be reusing bottles for your next batch, get labels that can be easily peeled off. There are self-adhesive, removable labels, e.g., Avery, or labels made from plain paper that you apply with a water-soluble glue or paste, which you can easily remove by running hot water over the label or by soaking bottles in a hot-water bath.

Print waterproof labels—that means, either print using a laser printer, or apply a spray varnish if printing using an inkjet printer so that the ink doesn't run off under humid conditions or when bottles are chilled in an ice bucket.

BOTTLING EQUIPMENT

You can get by with only basic, inexpensive equipment if you are bottling a standard carboy of wine, that is, 25 bottles at a time. As you grow your hobby, you'll likely want to upgrade to more efficient equipment.

Bottle Washer/Rinser

Like almost all novice winemakers, you'll be reusing bottles, and that means washing and sanitizing bottles come bottling day. A single-bottle washer/rinser (Figure 13.4a) installed on a laundry sink faucet will do the job just fine. It uses tap-water pressure to wash and rinse. You start and stop the flow of water by pushing and pressing the bottle against the built-in valve.

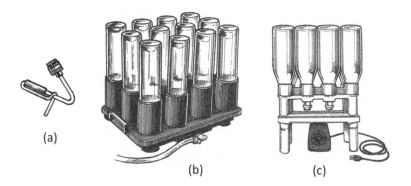

Figure 13.4: a) Single-bottle washer/rinser; b) 2-in-1 Bottle Washer; c) FastWasher

A 2-in-1 Bottle Washer (Figure 13.4b) or FastWasher (Figure 13.4c) can wash 12 bottles at a time and will speed things up when bottling several batches and many cases in a day. Each type of washer is placed in a deep sink. The 2-in-1 Bottle Washer connects to a faucet to deliver a strong jet of water to bottles, while the FastWasher uses a submersible pump to wash bottles.

Bottle Tree and Sanitizer

A "bottle tree" fitted with a bottle sanitizer (Figure 13.5) will come in handy when rinsing, sanitizing, and drip-drying bottles. Choose a model with stackable, modular bottle trays/posts to "grow the tree" as you expand

Figure 13.5: Bottle tree with bottle sanitizer

Figure 13.6: Bottling wand

your hobby. The bottle sanitizer, or sanitizer injector, is used to squirt a sanitizing solution into bottles—only one at a time.

Bottle Fillers

There are many types of bottle fillers to suit any budget and production volume. These operate either by gravity, or using a diaphragm or vacuum pump.

For bottling one carboy at a time, a gravity-fed bottling wand (Figure 13.6) works very well, though a bit more cumbersome if using bottles with a punt (the upward curve in the bottom of some bottles). The wand has a springless or spring-activated "foot valve" to control the flow of wine into a bottle and is connected to a hose and racking cane. To fill a bottle, first start the flow of wine (for the first bottle only) by sucking wine from the hose or using an auto-siphon racking tube, then attach the hose to the wand, insert in a bottle and push the valve open against the bottom to start filling. As the bottle fills, pull the wand out when the wine reaches the top of the bottle. The wine drops back down to the proper fill level to insert a standard cork into the bottle. If the wine drops too far down, press the wand tip just slightly against the top of the inside of the bottle to get the wine another ½ inch or so higher in level before corking.

The Ferrari Automatic Bottle Filler (Figure 13.7) is a gravity-fed filler also ideal for small batches. Here too you have to prime the filler by suction. Then, slide the filler on the bottle and press the button to start the flow of wine. It stops automatically at a preset adjustable level, and then you move to the next bottle.

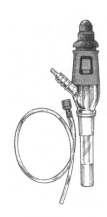

The Buon Vino Super Automatic Bottle Filler (Figure 13.8) is a gravity-fed filler, very similar in operation to the Ferrari Automatic Bottle Filler; it comes with a racking tube and tip. The filler head mechanism has a flow regulator, filler nozzle and overflow tube. Start the flow of wine by suction from the overflow tube. The nozzle has a diverter that pours wine down the glass of the bottle to limit agitation. The flow stops automatically at a preset adjustable level; excess wine

Figure 13.7: Ferrari Automatic Bottle Filler

goes into an overflow bottle. When a bottle is filled, move the filler to the next bottle and push down on the flow regulator to restart the flow of wine.

The Buon Vino Tabletop Electric Fill Jet (Figure 13.9) use a similar filler-head mechanism as the gravity-fed Super Automatic Bottle Filler, but it is powered by a self-priming diaphragm pump for faster bottling. The carboy

Figure 13.8: Buon Vino Super Automatic Bottle Filler

Figure 13.9: Buon Vino Tabletop Electric Fill Jet

to be bottled from can be at the same level as the filler, which means no lifting carboys onto a table or counter. Being a stationary filler, you move bottles in/out of the filler head; the operation is otherwise identical.

The All In One Wine Pump bottle filler (Figure 13.10) uses an electric vacuum pump to displace wine and fill bottles, one at a time, to a preset adjustable fill level using a stopper attachment that includes a vacuum valve to control the flow of wine down the side of the glass to minimize foaming. Overflow wine is sucked back into the carboy, and so, it must sit below bottles during the filling operation.

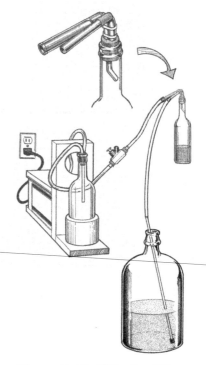

Figure 13.10: All In One Wine Pump bottle filler

The Tenco Enolmatic Bottle Filler (Figure 13.11) is a stationary-type tabletop filler that also uses an electric vacuum pump to displace wine and fill bottles, one at a time, to a preset adjustable fill level. It includes a vacuum valve to control the flow of wine down the side of the glass to minimize foaming. Overflow wine is sucked into a bowl part of the unit, the same bowl used

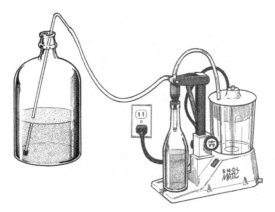

Figure 13.11: Enolmatic Bottle Filler

to create the vacuum and so, the carboy can be set at the same level as bottles during the filling operation.

Corker

There are two kinds of home winemaking corkers for inserting corks into standard 750-mL bottles: double-lever corker, and tabletop or floor corkers (Figure 13.12).

The double-lever corker works well for small batches and with no. 8 corks, if you decide to use those. You'll need a lot more mus-

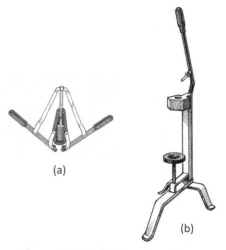

(a)

(b)

Figure 13.12: a) Manual corker; b) floor corker

cle power with no. 9 corks. It can be very hard to drive these in all the while keeping the bottle steady and pushing down on the corker. Micro-agglomerates are much too hard for this type of corker, and synthetic corks can get damaged during insertion and compromise the closure. You'll soon want to upgrade to a good tabletop or floor corker for anything more than a standard batch.

Tabletop or floor corkers are very efficient. The corker head has a set of crimping jaws that squeeze the cork, which gets inserted into a bottle when the lever is pulled down. The bottle support locks into position during corking to ensure flawless insertion.

Some models use plastic jaws, which tend to wear out rather quickly. If you intend to grow your hobby, go with a model with brass jaws, such as Italian (Ferrari in blue, others red) and Portuguese (smaller, red) corkers.

Adjust the corker so that the top of the cork is inserted flush with the top of the bottle for a clean finish.

THE BOTTLING PROCESS

It's bottling day! Your wine is ready to be bottled, you have all the necessary bottles, corks, capsules and labels, and you're very excited. You can certainly work on your own if bottling a single batch or if time and efficiency are not an issue. As you grow your hobby, you'll likely want to enlist friends and family to help out and speed things along.

First, wash and sanitize the required number of bottles and all bottling equipment using a sulfite–citric solution or other sanitizing agent. This will include the bottle filler, racking cane and hoses, corker jaws, pump, and anything else that will come in contact with wine. To sanitize bottles with a bottle sanitizer device, squirt some sanitizing solution into bottles a minimum of three times. Remember to sanitize your filter system if you are filtering in-line with your bottling. Let all equipment air-dry and bottles drip-dry on a bottle tree. You can rinse bottles after sanitizing if you have fresh, clean municipal water but this is optional if you use a compatible sanitizing agent. Refer back to the section SANITIZING in Chapter THREE on how to sanitize. And again, there is no need to soak or sanitize corks.

It seemed like washing and sanitizing took forever, but you're finally ready to bottle!

If you are filling bottles using a gravity-fed bottle filler, set the carboy higher up on a table or counter, prime the racking cane and hose, and attach to your bottle filler. Fill bottles so that you have ¼ to ½ inch of headspace. That is the space between the wine and the bottom of the cork in the bottle (Figure 13.13), which will allow for wine expansion and contraction during cellaring.

Insert corks, apply capsules and labels, and once done, store bottles upright for a few days if using natural-cork closures to allow the cork material to re-expand completely to its original shape and provide a good seal. Then you can store your bottles horizontally. If you are using agglomerate-type or synthetic corks, you can store bottles whichever way

Figure 13.13: Correct and incorrect headspace

you prefer, but allow 30 minutes for corks to properly seal against the neck of the bottles if you still intend on storing bottles horizontally.

CHAPTER FOURTEEN

Making a Lively White from Chardonnay

Here, we'll make a 5-gal (19-L) batch of light and refreshing, fruity dry white wine from grapes with 11%–12.5% ABV and 5–8 g/L TA that you can sweeten to taste and drink within 6–9 months. You can use fresh or sterile juice instead of grapes.

You can use any white grape variety you like. As an example, we'll use Chardonnay and ferment relatively cool, as cool as possible close to 55°F (13°C), without any oak influence so as not to detract from the fruity character we're after. If you cannot ferment at cool temperature, you may lose some of the fruity aromas. You can ferment warmer, at around 68°F (20°C), if you're partial to aromatic characteristics that some varieties such as Sauvignon Blanc and Gewürztraminer have to offer. We'll forego malolactic fermentation (MLF) so as not to drop acidity excessively and to prevent any malolactic-related by-products that may not suit this style of wine.

Be sure to process the press-run juice as quickly as possible and protect it from the elements to minimize the amount of oxygen absorbed, which could impact delicate fruity aromas.

Keep meticulous records of all your operations and measurements in a log book. You can download a log sheet at ModernHomeWinemaking.com.

INGREDIENTS

- ☐ 100 lbs (45 kg) grapes, Chardonnay or any white grape variety, or 6 gal (23 L) of fresh or sterile juice
- ☐ 1 lb (500 g) rice hulls (if needed for pressing)
- ☐ 2 tsp pectic enzymes
- ☐ One 5-g packet Lalvin QA23 yeast (or equivalent)
- ☐ 1 tsp yeast rehydration nutrients (e.g., Go-Ferm)
- ☐ 2 tsp complex yeast nutrients (e.g., Fermaid K), to be added in two steps
- ☐ Potassium metabisulfite (KMS) or Campden tablets
- ☐ 1 tsp bentonite
- ☐ Kieselsol–chitosan combo pack
- ☐ ½ tsp potassium sorbate (if sweetening or not fermenting dry)
- ☐ Table sugar (for sweetening, if desired)

EQUIPMENT

- ☐ Crusher[1,2]
- ☐ Press[2]
- ☐ Large vat[1,2] e.g., 13 gal (50 L)
- ☐ 6-gal (23-L) carboy
- ☐ 5-gal (19-L) carboy
- ☐ Racking cane and hose
- ☐ Airlock and bung
- ☐ Hydrometer and test cylinder
- ☐ Floating thermometer
- ☐ Acidity test kit
- ☐ pH meter
- ☐ 7.9-gal (30-L) pail
- ☐ Food-grade scoop
- ☐ Sieve
- ☐ Wine thief (or gravy baster)
- ☐ Long mixing spoon or lees stirrer
- ☐ Measuring cup
- ☐ Filtering equipment and pads/cartridges (optional)
- ☐ Bottling equipment

[1]Not required if whole-bunch pressing
[2]Not required if using juice

SUPPLIES

- ☐ Cleaner and sanitizer
- ☐ 25 bottles
- ☐ 25 corks
- ☐ 25 capsules
- ☐ 25 labels

STEP 1 – CRUSHING AND PRESSING

ⓘ *If using fresh juice which has not been cold settled, go to STEP 2 – COLD SETTLING.*

ⓘ *If using fresh, cold-settled juice or sterile juice, go to STEP 3 – JUICE ANALYSIS AND ADJUSTMENTS.*

ⓘ *Work in an area with cool ambient temperature as close as possible to 55°F (13°C).*

☐ **1.1** Clean and sanitize all equipment, tools, and fermentors.

☐ **1.2** Remove any leaves and other debris still in the grapes. Crush the grapes into a large vat and remove as many stems as possible as you crush. Immediately transfer the crushed grapes to the press using a large scoop.

Alternatively, directly transfer grape bunches to the press for whole-bunch pressing without crushing.

 You may find that certain grape varieties, such as Muscat and Niagara, have very slippery skins that can cause juice to not drain well out of the press. To improve drainage, evenly distribute 1 lb (500 g) of rice hulls into the crushed grapes as you load the press.

☐ **1.3** Place a sieve on the pail and slide under the spout of the press to catch any grape fragments while collecting juice. Press lightly and extract as much press-run juice as desired.

 The more pressure you exert to extract more juice, the more tannins you'll extract, which could detract from the desired style of wine.

Unload the press and discard the pomace to the compost.

☐ **1.4** Dissolve ¼ tsp KMS or 4 crushed Campden tablets in 100 mL of *cool* water, add to the juice and stir thoroughly.

☐ **1.5** Dissolve 2 tsp of pectic enzymes in 100 mL of *cold* water, and stir into the juice. Place the lid on the pail and shut tightly.

STEP 2 – COLD SETTLING

☐ **2.1** Transfer the pail of juice to the refrigerator or the coldest area you can manage, down to 45°F (8°C), or colder, if possible. Let stand 24 hours to cold settle and to let grape residues and other heavy particulates fall to the bottom.

☐ **2.2** Once cold settled, take the pail out of the refrigerator and gently transfer to your cool cellar or fermentation area, set it on a table or shelf, and let it warm up. You'll ferment at around or as close as possible to 55°F (13°C).

☐ **2.3** Open the pail and carefully rack 5 gallons (19 liters) of the juice to a 6-gal (23-L) carboy.

If you have 6 gal (23 L) of juice, rack instead to another pail to allow for foaming during primary fermentation as the 6-gal (23-L) carboy would be too small.

STEP 3 – JUICE ANALYSIS AND ADJUSTMENTS

TARGETS   PA: 11%–12.5%   SG: 1.082–1.094   TA: 5–10 g/L   pH: 3.1–3.4

☐ **3.1** Take a sample of the juice using your sanitized wine thief. Measure and record temperature, SG, TA and pH.

Also sanitize your hydrometer and test cylinder as you'll likely want to return the sample to the carboy or pail.

☐ **3.2** Make any adjustments based on desired targets.

STEP 4 – PRIMARY FERMENTATION

ⓘ *Set the temperature of your winemaking area to be able to ferment at around or as close as possible to 55°F (13°C) keeping in mind that fermentation will generate some heat, about 5°F–10°F (3°C–5°C). Don't worry if you can't achieve such low temperatures.*

ⓘ *Primary fermentation will take at least 7 days and up to 2 weeks or more depending on temperature; the colder, the longer.*

ⓘ *Always place the airlock and bung on the carboy (or loose lid on the pail) after any operation.*

☐ **4.1**   Prepare the yeast starter. Slowly add 1 tsp of yeast rehydration nutrients to 100 mL of fresh, chlorine-free water at around 110°F (43°C) in a measuring cup, stir thoroughly until well dissolved, let cool down to 105°F (40°C), then add one 5-g packet of Lalvin QA23 yeast (or equivalent) while stirring *very gently*, and let hydrate for approximately 20 minutes.

☐ **4.2**   Measure the temperature of the juice and yeast starter. Add the yeast starter directly to the juice if the difference in temperature between the juice and yeast starter is less than 18°F (10°C); otherwise, acclimate the yeast doing step additions of juice prior to adding it to the whole batch (see *Preparing the Yeast Culture and Inoculating the Juice* in the section CONDUCTING AND MONITORING FERMENTATION in Chapter SIX on p. 98).

☐ **4.3**   6–12 hours after adding the yeast starter, dissolve 1 tsp of complex yeast nutrients in about 50 mL of warm water, and stir into the juice until well dispersed. You can place a floating thermometer in the juice at this point.

☐ **4.4**   Prepare a bentonite solution by *slowly* adding 1 tsp of bentonite in about 100 mL of *hot* water in a container with lid and let rehydrate for 12–24 hours; periodically shake the solution vigorously until ready to add to the juice.

☐ **4.5**   Within 24–36 hours of inoculation, you should see signs of fermentation with bubbles rising towards the surface of the juice. Slowly stir in the bentonite solution; continue stirring gently until well dispersed.

☐ **4.6**   During fermentation, measure and record temperature and SG every day to make sure all is proceeding well. Also stir the wine thoroughly but very gently to avoid causing an eruption.

☐ **4.7**   When SG has dropped about 30 points to between 1.050 and 1.060, dissolve 1 tsp of complex yeast nutrients in about 50 mL of warm water, and stir into the wine until well dispersed.

STEP 5 – SECONDARY FERMENTATION

TARGET   SG: 1.010–1.020

ⓘ *Secondary fermentation will take another 7 days or more depending on temperature.*

☐ **5.1**   When SG is in the target range, stir the wine to re-suspend sediment, and rack to a sanitized 5-gal (19-L) carboy using a racking cane and hose. Place a bung and airlock with sulfite solution on the carboy.

☐ **5.2**   Ferment to complete dryness, that is, until SG is at or below 0.995 with a steady reading for at least two consecutive days.

STEP 6 – RACKING AND DEGASSING

TARGETS   SG: 0.995 or less   TA: 5–8 g/L   pH: 3.1–3.4

 If you wish to skip degassing, go to step 6.3. Degassing is only necessary if you expect to bottle the wine quickly, say, within 6 months, or if you don't expect the wine will degas sufficiently on its own.

☐ **6.1**   Rack the wine to a sanitized pail or 6-gal (23-L) carboy to allow for sufficient headspace for foaming during degassing, being careful not to pick up any lees. Let the wine splash during racking to help release some gas.

☐ **6.2**   Degas the wine until it stops foaming; use a long mixing spoon or lees stirrer installed on a drill.

☐ **6.3**   Take a sample using your wine thief, degas the sample (if required), and measure and record the final SG, TA and pH. Also smell and taste the wine to see how you like it and to make sure it has not developed any undesirable smells or flavors.

☐ **6.4**   If working in a pail, rack the wine to a sanitized 5-gal (19-L) carboy, and top up with a similar wine, if required; if a similar wine is not available, water is fine if only a small amount is needed, otherwise, it can overly dilute the wine. Place the airlock and bung back on the carboy.

Store the wine as cool as possible to around 55°F (13°C) from here on. Try not to exceed 68°F (20°C), which could otherwise shorten the life of the wine.

STEP 7 – CLARIFICATION AND STABILIZATION

TARGETS   TA: 5–8 g/L   pH: 3.1–3.4

ⓘ *Be sure to place the airlock and bung back on the carboy after each step.*

☐ **7.1**   Dissolve ¼ tsp KMS or 4 crushed Campden tablets in cool water, and gently stir into the wine.

You can proceed to step 7.2 now or anytime up to several months later. If aging, add sulfite every 3 months; dissolve ⅛ tsp KMS or 2 crushed Campden tablets in cool water, and gently stir into the wine.

☐ **7.2**   Add the packet of Kieselsol suspension while stirring continuously for about 2 minutes.

☐ **7.3**   The next day, add the packet of chitosan and stir thoroughly for about 2 minutes.

☐ **7.4**   Let the wine stand until completely clear.

☐ **7.5**   Transfer the carboy to the refrigerator for cold stabilization, and hold for at least 2 weeks.

☐ **7.6**   Take the wine out and return to the cellar, rack to another sanitized carboy, and top up.

☐ **7.7**   Take a sample of wine using your wine thief, and measure TA and pH once again and taste the wine to assess the impact of cold stabilization.

If cold stabilization is not possible, you can add a stabilizer that inhibits tartrates (see the section TARTRATES in Chapter NINE). Be sure to first rack the wine into another carboy.

STEP 8 – SWEETENING (IF DESIRED)

ⓘ *If final SG is not 0.995 or lower, or as a precaution, stabilize the wine before adding fermentable sugar. Alternatively, you can forego the use of sulfite and sorbate by using a non-fermentable sweetener, such as stevia, and skip to step 8.4.*

☐ **8.1** Dissolve ¼ tsp KMS or 4 crushed Campden tablets in cool water, and gently stir into the wine.

☐ **8.2** Dissolve ½ tsp of potassium sorbate in 50 mL of cool water, and add to the carboy while stirring continuously.

☐ **8.3** Let stand for approximately 2 weeks to make sure no sediment forms.

☐ **8.4** Sweeten to taste with table sugar, wine conditioner, or your favorite sweetener as per your bench trials. Add the sweetener in small increments and stir until well dissolved, taste the wine, and repeat as desired until you hit your sweet spot or as per bench trials.

STEP 9 – FILTERING (OPTIONAL)

ⓘ *Filtering is only required if the wine shows any slight haze or if you want a crystal clear appearance.*

☐ **9.1** Clean and sanitize all filtering equipment, including hoses, and pads or cartridges.

☐ **9.2** If there is any haze, first filter with no. 1 or AF1/AF2 pads or a 10-micron cartridge into another carboy. You can skip this coarse filtering if the wine is clear. Rinse the first carboy.

☐ **9.3** Filter with no. 2 or AF3 pads or a 5-micron cartridge back into the first carboy. Rinse the other carboy.

☐ **9.4** Filter with no. 3 or AF4 pads or a 1-micron cartridge into the other carboy. You'll likely have "lost" about half a bottle's worth of wine, and so, top up accordingly, and place the airlock and bung back on the carboy.

STEP 10 – BOTTLING

☐ **10.1** When ready to bottle, first dissolve ¼ tsp KMS or 4 crushed Campden tablets in cool water, and gently stir into the wine, and then proceed with bottling.

☐ **10.2** Clean and sanitize bottles and all bottling equipment.

☐ **10.3** Fill bottles, cork each bottle as soon as filled, and apply capsules and labels.

☐ **10.4** Store bottles right side up for a few days, then store horizontally in a cool cellar.

 Wait at least 1 week, perhaps more, especially if you've filtered the wine, to allow the wine to settle and get over bottle shock so that it tastes as it did before bottling.

☐ **10.5** You can bottle age some more as the wine will slowly improve over the next few months.

☐ **10.6** Enjoy!

CHAPTER FIFTEEN

Making a Fruity Rosé from Grenache

*H*ere, we'll make a 5-gal (19-L) batch of medium-bodied, fruity dry rosé wine from grapes with 12%–13% ABV and 5–8 g/L TA that you can sweeten to taste and drink within 6–9 months. You can use fresh or sterile rosé juice instead of grapes.

You can use any white-fleshed, red-skinned grape variety you like. Color is extracted from skins by "macerating," that is, by soaking crushed grapes in their juice for just a short duration. If using a richly colored variety, you can skip maceration and press crushed grapes or whole-bunch grapes to avoid the risk of extracting too much color and ending up with a light red wine instead.

Aglianico, Barbera, Catawba, Grenache, Léon Millot, Merlot, Mourvèdre, Pinot Noir, Pinotage, Sangiovese, Tempranillo, and Zinfandel are all great choices for macerating while Marquette (a teinturier), Petite Sirah, and Syrah are excellent choices as well, although these should go straight to the press without any crushing and maceration.

We'll use a most popular variety, Grenache, also known as Garnacha, as an example, with a short maceration to make a medium-bodied, fruity-style rosé, and, as with our white wine in Chapter FOURTEEN, ferment relatively cool with no malolactic fermentation (MLF) and no oak influence. If you cannot ferment at cool temperature, you may lose some of the fruity aromas. You can ferment warmer, at around 68°F (20°C), if you are looking for greater varietal expression.

INGREDIENTS

- ☐ 100 lbs (45 kg) grapes, Grenache or other red grape variety, or 6 gal (23 L) of fresh or sterile rosé juice
- ☐ 1 lb (500 g) rice hulls (if needed for pressing)
- ☐ 2 tsp pectic enzymes
- ☐ One 5-g packet Lalvin 71B-1122 yeast (or equivalent)
- ☐ 1 tsp yeast rehydration nutrients (e.g., Go-Ferm)
- ☐ 2 tsp complex yeast nutrients (e.g., Fermaid K), to be added in two steps
- ☐ Potassium metabisulfite (KMS) or Campden tablets
- ☐ 1 tsp bentonite
- ☐ Kieselsol–chitosan combo pack
- ☐ ½ tsp potassium sorbate (if sweetening or not fermenting dry)
- ☐ Table sugar (for sweetening, if desired)

EQUIPMENT

- ☐ Crusher[1,2]
- ☐ Press[2]
- ☐ Large vat[1,2] e.g., 13 gal (50 L)
- ☐ 7.9-gal (30-L) pail
- ☐ 6-gal (23-L) carboy
- ☐ 5-gal (19-L) carboy
- ☐ Punchdown tool or potato masher
- ☐ Tarp
- ☐ Racking cane and hose
- ☐ Airlock and bung
- ☐ Hydrometer and test cylinder
- ☐ Floating thermometer
- ☐ Acidity test kit
- ☐ pH meter
- ☐ Food-grade scoop
- ☐ Sieve
- ☐ Wine thief (or gravy baster)
- ☐ Long mixing spoon or lees stirrer
- ☐ Measuring cup
- ☐ Filtering equipment and pads/cartridges (optional)
- ☐ Bottling equipment

[1]Not required if whole-bunch pressing
[2]Not required if using juice

SUPPLIES

- ☐ Cleaner and sanitizer
- ☐ 25 bottles
- ☐ 25 corks
- ☐ 25 capsules
- ☐ 25 labels

The process is almost identical to making white wine except for color extraction. If you macerate, you'll also extract some tannins. Those are okay in the style we're after here—just be careful not to over-extract as excessive tannins will clash with the higher acidity in this style of wine. The red hues will turn towards an orange color with oxygen exposure so, if you're partial to more of a red color, try and limit air exposure as much as possible while you work the wine.

Keep meticulous records of all your operations and measurements in a log book. You can download a log sheet at <u>ModernHomeWinemaking.com</u>.

STEP 1 – CRUSHING

ⓘ *If using fresh juice which has not been cold settled, go to STEP 4 – COLD SETTLING.*

ⓘ *If using fresh, cold-settled juice or sterile juice, go to STEP 5 – JUICE ANALYSIS AND ADJUSTMENTS.*

ⓘ *Work in an area with cool ambient temperature as close as possible to 55°F (13°C).*

☐ **1.1** Clean and sanitize all equipment, tools, and fermentors.

☐ **1.2** Remove any leaves and other debris still in the grapes. Crush the grapes into a large vat and remove as many stems as possible as you crush.

Alternatively, directly transfer grape bunches to the press for whole-bunch pressing without crushing and proceed to STEP 3 – PRESSING.

☐ **1.3** Mix thoroughly the load of crushed grapes with a punchdown tool (or potato masher).

☐ **1.4** Dissolve ¼ tsp KMS or 4 crushed Campden tablets in 100 mL of *cool* water, add to the load of grapes, mix thoroughly with a punchdown tool, and place a heavy tarp on the vat to protect the load from the elements and fruit flies.

STEP 2 – MACERATION

☐ **2.1**   Monitor color extraction by checking at least once an hour. Extract more color than desired as there will be some significant color loss during fermentation and post processing. How long you macerate to achieve your color depends on the state of the grapes (and variety, if other than Grenache), temperature, and of course, your desired color. It can take as little as 2 hours to as much as 12 or even 24 hours. Also periodically stir the grape solids and juice with a punchdown tool.

Proceed to the next step when you have achieved your desired color.

STEP 3 – PRESSING

☐ **3.1**   If your vat is equipped with a bottom valve and sieve, drain as much of the free-run juice available into a pail. Transfer the crushed grapes to the press using a large scoop.

If not macerating, simply load whole bunches into the press.

 You may find that certain grape varieties, such as Catawba and Concord, have very slippery skins that can cause juice to not drain well out of the press. To improve drainage, evenly distribute 1 lb (500 g) of rice hulls into the crushed grapes as you load the press.

☐ **3.2**   Place a sieve on the pail and slide under the spout of the press to catch any grape fragments while collecting juice. Press lightly and extract as much press-run juice as desired.

 The more pressure you exert to extract more juice, the more tannins you'll extract, which could detract from the desired style of wine.

Unload the press and discard the pomace to the compost.

☐ **3.3**   Dissolve 2 tsp of pectic enzymes in 100 mL of *cold* water, and stir into the juice. Place the lid on the pail and shut tight.

STEP 4 – COLD SETTLING

☐ **4.1** Transfer the pail of juice to the refrigerator or the coldest area you can manage, down to 45°F (8°C), or colder, if possible. Let stand 24 hours to cold settle and to let grape residues and other heavy particulates fall to the bottom.

☐ **4.2** Once cold settled, take the pail out of the refrigerator and gently transfer to your cool cellar or fermentation area, set it on a table or shelf, and let it warm up. You'll ferment at around or as close as possible to 55°F (13°C).

☐ **4.3** Open the pail and carefully rack 5 gallons (19 liters) of the juice to a 6-gal (23-L) carboy.

 If you have 6 gal (23 L) of juice, rack instead to another pail to allow for foaming during primary fermentation as the 6-gal (23-L) carboy would be too small.

STEP 5 – JUICE ANALYSIS AND ADJUSTMENTS

TARGETS   PA: 12%–13%   SG: 1.090–1.098   TA: 5–10 g/L   pH: 3.1–3.4

☐ **5.1** Take a sample of juice using your sanitized wine thief. Measure and record temperature, SG, TA and pH.

 Also sanitize your hydrometer and test cylinder as you'll likely want to return the sample to the carboy or pail.

☐ **5.2** Make any adjustments based on desired targets.

STEP 6 – PRIMARY FERMENTATION

ⓘ *Set the temperature of your winemaking area to be able to ferment at around or as close as possible to 55°F (13°C) keeping in mind that fermentation will generate some heat, about 5°F–10°F (3°C–5°C). Don't worry if you can't achieve such low temperatures.*

ⓘ *Primary fermentation will take at least 7 days and up to 2 weeks or more depending on temperature; the colder, the longer.*

ⓘ *Always place the airlock and bung on the carboy (or loose lid on the pail) after any operation.*

☐ **6.1** Prepare the yeast starter. Slowly add 1 tsp of yeast rehydration nutrients to 100 mL of fresh, chlorine-free water at around 110°F (43°C) in a measuring cup, stir thoroughly until well dissolved, let cool down to 105°F (40°C), then add one 5-g packet of Lalvin 71B-1122 yeast (or equivalent) while *very gently* stirring, and let hydrate for approximately 20 minutes.

☐ **6.2** Measure the temperature of the juice and yeast starter. Add the yeast starter directly to the juice if the difference in temperature between the juice and yeast starter is less than 18°F (10°C); otherwise, acclimate the yeast doing step additions of juice prior to adding it to the whole batch (see *Preparing the Yeast Culture and Inoculating the Juice* in the section on CONDUCTING AND MONITORING FERMENTATION in Chapter SIX on p. 98).

☐ **6.3** 6–12 hours after adding the yeast starter, dissolve 1 tsp of complex yeast nutrients in about 50 mL of warm water, and stir into the juice until well dispersed. You can place a floating thermometer in the juice at this point.

☐ **6.4** Prepare a bentonite solution by *slowly* adding 1 tsp of bentonite in about 100 mL of *hot* water in a container with lid and let rehydrate for 12–24 hours; periodically shake the solution vigorously until ready to add to the juice.

☐ **6.5** Within 24–36 hours of inoculation, you should see signs of fermentation with bubbles rising towards the surface of the juice. Slowly stir in the bentonite solution; continue stirring gently until well dispersed.

☐ **6.6** During fermentation, measure and record temperature and SG every day to make sure all is proceeding well. Also stir the wine thoroughly but very gently to avoid causing an eruption.

☐ **6.7** When SG has dropped about 40 points to between 1.050 and 1.060, dissolve 1 tsp of complex yeast nutrients in about 50 mL of warm water, and stir into the wine until well dispersed.

STEP 7 – SECONDARY FERMENTATION

TARGETS   SG: 1.010–1.020

ⓘ *Secondary fermentation will take another 7 days or more depending on temperature.*

☐ **7.1**   When SG is in the target range, stir the wine to re-suspend sediment, and rack to a sanitized 5-gal (19-L) carboy using a racking cane and hose. Place a bung and airlock with sulfite solution on the carboy.

☐ **7.2**   Ferment to complete dryness, that is, until SG is at or below 0.995 with a steady reading for at least two consecutive days.

STEP 8 – RACKING AND DEGASSING

TARGETS   SG: 0.995 or less   TA: 5–8 g/L   pH: 3.1–3.4

 If you wish to skip degassing, jump to step 8.3. Degassing is only necessary if you expect to bottle the wine quickly, say, within 6 months, or if you don't expect the wine will degas sufficiently on its own.

☐ **8.1**   Rack the wine to a sanitized pail or 6-gal (23-L) carboy to allow for sufficient headspace for foaming during degassing, being careful not to pick up any lees. Let the wine splash during racking to help release some gas.

☐ **8.2**   Degas the wine until it stops foaming; use a long mixing spoon or lees stirrer installed on a drill.

☐ **8.3**   Take a sample using your wine thief, degas the sample (if required), and measure and record the final SG, TA and pH. Also smell and taste the wine to see how you like it and to make sure it has not developed any undesirable smells or flavors.

☐ **8.4**   If working in a pail, rack the wine to a sanitized 5-gal (19-L) carboy, and top up with a similar wine, if required; if a similar wine is not available, water is fine if only a small amount is needed, otherwise, it can overly dilute the wine. Place the airlock and bung back on the carboy.

Store the wine as cool as possible to around 55°F (13°C) from here on. Try not to exceed 68°F (20°C), which could otherwise shorten the life of the wine.

STEP 9 – CLARIFICATION AND STABILIZATION

TARGETS   TA: 5–8 g/L   pH: 3.1–3.4

ⓘ *Be sure to place the airlock and bung back on the carboy after each step.*

☐ **9.1** Dissolve ¼ tsp KMS or 4 crushed Campden tablets in cool water, and gently stir into the wine.

 You can proceed to step 9.2 now or anytime up to several months later. If aging, add sulfite every 3 months; dissolve ⅛ tsp KMS or 2 crushed Campden tablets in cool water, and gently stir into the wine.

☐ **9.2** Add the packet of Kieselsol suspension while stirring continuously for about 2 minutes.

☐ **9.3** The next day, add the packet of chitosan and stir thoroughly for about 2 minutes.

☐ **9.4** Let the wine stand until completely clear.

☐ **9.5** Transfer the carboy to the refrigerator for cold stabilization, and hold for at least 2 weeks.

☐ **9.6** Take the wine out and return to the cellar, rack to another sanitized carboy, and top up.

☐ **9.7** Take a sample of wine using your wine thief, and measure TA and pH once again and taste the wine to assess the impact of cold stabilization.

 If cold stabilization is not possible, you can add a stabilizer that inhibits tartrates (see the section TARTRATES in Chapter NINE). Be sure to first rack the wine into another carboy.

STEP 10 – SWEETENING (IF DESIRED)

ⓘ *If final SG is not 0.995 or lower, or as a precaution, stabilize the wine before adding fermentable sugar. Alternatively, you can forego the use of sulfite and sorbate by using a non-fermentable sweetener, such as stevia, and skip to step 10.4.*

☐ **10.1** Dissolve ¼ tsp KMS or 4 crushed Campden tablets in cool water, and gently stir into the wine.

☐ **10.2** Dissolve ½ tsp of potassium sorbate in 50 mL of cool water, and add to the carboy while stirring continuously.

☐ **10.3** Let stand for approximately 2 weeks to make sure no sediment forms.

☐ **10.4** Sweeten to taste with table sugar, wine conditioner, or your favorite sweetener as per your bench trials. Add the sweetener in small increments and stir until well dissolved, taste the wine, and repeat as desired until you hit your sweet spot or as per bench trials.

STEP 11 – FILTERING (OPTIONAL)

ⓘ *Filtering is only required if the wine shows any slight haze or if you want a crystal clear appearance.*

☐ **11.1** Clean and sanitize all filtering equipment, including hoses, and pads or cartridges.

☐ **11.2** If there is any haze, first filter with no. 1 or AF1/AF2 pads or a 10-micron cartridge into another carboy. You can skip this coarse filtering if the wine is clear. Rinse the first carboy.

☐ **11.3** Filter with no. 2 or AF3 pads or a 5-micron cartridge back into the first carboy. Rinse the other carboy.

☐ **11.4** Filter with no. 3 or AF4 pads or a 1-micron cartridge into the other carboy. You will likely have "lost" about half a bottle's worth of wine, and so, top up accordingly, and place the bung and airlock back on the carboy.

STEP 12 – BOTTLING

☐ **12.1** When ready to bottle, first dissolve ¼ tsp KMS or 4 crushed Campden tablets in cool water, and gently stir into the wine, and then proceed with bottling.

☐ **12.2** Clean and sanitize bottles and all bottling equipment.

☐ **12.3** Fill bottles, cork each bottle as soon as filled, and apply capsules and labels.

☐ **12.4** Store bottles right side up for a few days, then store horizontally in a cool cellar.

Wait at least 1 week, perhaps more, especially if you've filtered the wine, to allow the wine to settle and get over bottle shock so that it tastes as it did before bottling.

☐ **12.5** You can bottle age some more as the wine will slowly improve over the next few months.

☐ **12.6** Enjoy!

CHAPTER SIXTEEN

Making a Full-Bodied Red from Cabernet

*H*ere, we'll make a 5-gal (19-L) batch of premium, full-bodied, oaked dry red wine from grapes with 13%–14.5% ABV and 4–6 g/L TA that you can start drinking in about 18 months, although it will continue improving while aging and which will reward you with greater aromas and flavors years down the road.

You can use any red-skinned grape variety you like, with either red or white flesh inside. There are many to choose from, from Aglianico to Cabernet and Merlot to Zinfandel in European varieties, and Baco Noir to Frontenac and Norton in Native American varieties and hybrids. Alicante Bouschet and Marquette are examples of red-fleshed varieties, or teinturiers.

Color is extracted from skins by "macerating," that is, by soaking crushed grapes in their juice for days or even weeks. If you prefer not to work with grapes and not have to macerate and press, you'll find fresh, ready-to-ferment red juice, and even 100% pasteurized (sterile) pure juice and concentrate with a separate crushed-grapes pack that you can add to extract more color and tannins for a fuller-bodied style.

For our example, we'll use Cabernet Sauvignon with full maceration, meaning, until fermentation completes, we'll keep the wine on the skins, ferment relatively "hot" and do lots of punchdowns (Figure 16.1) to maximize color extraction. We'll also use oak chips or sticks. These will all contribute towards making a full-bodied red with oak influence worthy of aging. Color extraction can sometimes be a challenge in this variety, especially if the fruit is underripe.

INGREDIENTS

- ☐ 100 lbs (45 kg) grapes, Cabernet Sauvignon or other red grape variety, or 6 gal (23 L) of fresh or sterile juice
- ☐ 1 lb (500 g) rice hulls (if needed for pressing)
- ☐ 2 tsp pectic enzymes
- ☐ ½ cup untoasted oak powder
- ☐ 1 tbsp grape tannins
- ☐ 1½ tsp Lallemand Opti-Red
- ☐ Two 5-g packets Lalvin RC-212 yeast (or equivalent)
- ☐ 2 tsp yeast rehydration nutrients (e.g., Go-Ferm)
- ☐ 4 tsp complex yeast nutrients (e.g., Fermaid K), to be added in two steps
- ☐ 1 tsp malolactic nutrients (e.g., Opti-Malo Plus)
- ☐ One 125-mL pack Wyeast 4007 Malolactic Culture, or one 35-mL pack of White Labs WLP675 Malolactic Culture
- ☐ 1 cup medium-toast (MT) oak chips or one (1) MT oak stick
- ☐ Potassium metabisulfite (KMS) or Campden tablets
- ☐ Kieselsol–chitosan combo pack

EQUIPMENT

- ☐ Crusher[1]
- ☐ Press[1]
- ☐ Large vat[1] e.g., 13 gal (50 L)
- ☐ 7.9-gal (30-L) pail
- ☐ 6-gal (23-L) carboy
- ☐ 5-gal (19-L) carboy
- ☐ Punchdown tool or potato masher
- ☐ Tarp
- ☐ Racking cane and hose
- ☐ Airlock and bung
- ☐ Hydrometer and test cylinder
- ☐ Floating thermometer
- ☐ Acidity test kit
- ☐ pH meter
- ☐ Paper chromatography kit
- ☐ Food-grade scoop
- ☐ Sieve
- ☐ Wine thief (or gravy baster)
- ☐ Long mixing spoon or lees stirrer
- ☐ Large funnel
- ☐ Infusion tube for oak chips
- ☐ Measuring cup
- ☐ Filtering equipment and pads/cartridges (optional)
- ☐ Bottling equipment

[1]Not required if using juice

SUPPLIES

- ☐ Cleaner and sanitizer
- ☐ 25 bottles
- ☐ 25 corks
- ☐ 25 capsules
- ☐ 25 labels

To help stabilize color and also to build structure, we'll make use of Opti-Red, a Lallemand specific inactivated yeast product (see the section on COLOR STABILITY, MOUTHFEEL, AND OAK in Chapter FOUR), which you should be able to find repackaged in a small format—it's worth looking for it. We'll also reduce acidity by malolactic fermentation (MLF), which we'll launch sequentially after completion of alcoholic fermentation and pressing. We'll also let the wine

Figure 16.1: Punching down the cap

degas naturally using time and normal processing operations. Since we're going for a totally dry style here, we won't sweeten.

Keep meticulous records of all your operations and measurements in a log book. You can download a log sheet at <u>ModernHomeWinemaking.com</u>.

STEP 1 – CRUSHING

ⓘ *If using fresh or sterile juice, go to STEP 2 – JUICE ANALYSIS AND ADJUSTMENTS*

ⓘ *Work in an area with ambient temperature at around 68°F (20°C).*

☐ **1.1** Clean and sanitize all equipment, tools, and fermentors.

☐ **1.2** Remove any leaves and other debris still in the grapes. Crush the grapes into a large vat and remove as many stems as possible as you crush.

☐ **1.3** Dissolve 2 tsp pectic enzymes in 100 mL of *cold* water, distribute over the load of crushed grapes and mix well with a punchdown tool (or potato masher). Place a heavy tarp or lid on the vat or fermentor to protect from the elements and to keep fruit flies out. Wait 6–8 hours to allow the pectic enzymes to do their work before proceeding to step 1.4.

☐ **1.4** Distribute ½ cup of untoasted oak powder over the entire surface of crushed grapes, and mix well with a punchdown tool.

☐ **1.5** Dissolve 1½ tsp of Opti-Red powder in 100 mL of water, distribute over the entire surface of crushed grapes, and mix well with a punchdown tool.

☐ **1.6** Dissolve ¼ tsp KMS or 4 crushed Campden tablets in 100 mL of *cool* water, add to the load of crushed grapes, mix thoroughly with a punchdown tool, and place a heavy tarp on the vat to protect the load from the elements and fruit flies.

STEP 2 – JUICE ANALYSIS AND ADJUSTMENTS

TARGETS   PA: 13%–14.5%   SG: 1.100–1.110   TA: 4–7 g/L   pH: 3.3–3.6

☐ **2.1** Take a sample of juice using your sanitized wine thief, and measure and record temperature, SG, TA and pH.

Also sanitize your hydrometer and test cylinder as you'll likely want to return the sample to the carboy or pail.

☐ **2.2** Make any adjustments based on desired targets.

STEP 3 – MACERATION AND FERMENTATION

ⓘ *Fermentation will take 5–7 days or more depending on temperature.*

ⓘ *Place the tarp or lid back on top of the vat or pail after every operation and punchdown.*

☐ **3.1** Measure the temperature of the crushed grapes or juice; it should be at least at 68°F (20°C), if not, adjust room temperature and wait until the grapes or juice reach the desired temperature.

☐ **3.2** Prepare the yeast starter. Slowly add 2 tsp of yeast rehydration nutrients to 200 mL of fresh, chlorine-free water at around 110°F (43°C) in a measuring cup, stir thoroughly until well dissolved, let cool down to 105°F (40°C), then add two 5-g packets of Lalvin RC-212 yeast (or equivalent) while *very gently* stirring, and let hydrate for approximately 20 minutes.

☐ 3.3   Measure the temperature of the yeast starter and crushed grapes or juice. Add the yeast starter directly to the vat if the difference in temperature between the yeast starter and crushed grapes or juice is less than 18°F (10°C); otherwise, first acclimate the yeast doing step additions of juice (see *Preparing the Yeast Culture and Inoculating the Juice* in the section on CONDUCTING AND MONITORING FERMENTATION in Chapter SIX on p. 98), then add. Mix well using a punchdown tool.

☐ 3.4   6–12 hours after adding the yeast starter, thoroughly dissolve 2 tsp of complex yeast nutrients in about 100 mL of warm water, and mix into the vat using a punchdown tool until well dispersed.

☐ 3.5   Within 24–36 hours of inoculation, you should see signs of fermentation with bubbles rising towards the surface of the crushed grapes and juice. Keep doing punchdowns every 6 hours.

☐ 3.6   As fermentation becomes more vigorous, it will generate a lot of carbon dioxide (CO_2) gas, which will push the grape solids up to the surface and cause a thick layer, called a cap, to form. Punch down the cap and mix thoroughly into the wine 3–4 times per day using a punchdown tool, being sure to reach the bottom of the vat. *Never let the cap go dry.*

Fermentation and punchdowns will cause seeds to become free and fall to the bottom of the vat. Don't crush or mix the seeds during punchdowns.

During fermentation, measure and record temperature and SG every day to make sure all is proceeding well. Also, smell the wine to make sure that no off aromas or flavors are developing. Be particularly mindful when using underripe fruit or Native American varieties or hybrids prone to developing off aromas and flavors, particularly green, bell pepper-like aromas. If you detect any off aromas or flavors, proceed immediately to STEP 4 – PRESSING.

☐ 3.7   When SG has dropped about 30 points to between 1.070 and 1.080, dissolve 2 tsp of complex yeast nutrients in about 100 mL of warm water, do a punchdown, then distribute the rehydrated yeast nutrients over the entire surface and mix again until well dispersed using a punchdown tool.

☐ **3.8**   When SG has dropped to between 1.020 and 1.030, do a punch-down, then distribute 1 tbsp of grape tannins directly over the surface and mix again using a punchdown tool.

☐ **3.9**   Ferment to complete dryness, that is, until SG is at or below 0.995 with a steady reading for at least two consecutive days.

 The cap will break up and the grape solids will fall back into the wine, which can make it more difficult to separate the wine and grape solids for transfer to the press. You can scoop up the grape solids and transfer them to the press towards the end of fermentation but when there is still a cap, for example, when SG is at around 1.005.

STEP 4 – PRESSING

TARGET   SG: 0.995 or less

☐ **4.1**   If your vat is equipped with a bottom valve and sieve, drain as much of the free-run wine into a pail. Transfer the crushed grapes to the press using a large scoop. Do *not* transfer seeds.

 You may find that certain grape varieties, particularly those with thick skins, don't drain the wine well out of the press. To improve drainage, evenly distribute 1 lb (500 g) of rice hulls into the crushed and fermented grapes as you load the press.

☐ **4.2**   Place a sieve on the pail and slide under the spout of the press to catch any grape fragments and seeds. Press lightly and extract as much press-run wine as desired.

 While pressing, taste the wine to see if and when you detect a change. The more pressure you exert to extract more wine, the more green, harsh tannins you'll extract. If you detect a difference, measure pH too. Press-run wine may become a bit harsher and color may lose intensity and become less stable as pH increases. If so, you may want to treat free- and press-run wines separately, if you have the extra carboy capacity. If you are making single-carboy batches, you may not have much choice but to blend free- and press-run wines to keep the carboy full. If you decide to keep them separate, just be mindful that you'll have to manage two batches, which, for example, means managing two malolactic fermentations in STEP 6 below.

You can leave the wine in the pail and simply loosely place the lid on, or you can transfer it to a 6-gal (23-L) carboy using a large funnel and then secure with an airlock and bung.

Unload the press and discard the pomace to the compost.

☐ **4.3** Let the wine stand for 2–3 days to let the gross lees settle. Never exceed 3 days.

STEP 5 – FIRST RACKING

TARGETS   SG: 0.995 or less   TA: 4–6 g/L   pH: 3.3–3.6

ⓘ *The timing and execution of this first racking is very important to avoid hydrogen sulfide (H_2S) and a stinky rotten-egg smell to form.*

☐ **5.1** Open the pail or carboy and carefully rack the wine to a sanitized 5-gal (19-L) carboy being careful not to pick up gross lees.

☐ **5.2** Take a sample using your wine thief, measure and record the final SG, TA and pH. Also smell and taste the wine to see how you like it and to make sure it has not developed any undesirable smells or flavors. Secure the carboy with an airlock and bung until ready for the next step.

STEP 6 – MALOLACTIC FERMENTATION (MLF)

TARGETS   TA: 4–6 g/L   pH: 3.3–3.6

ⓘ *Until MLF completes, keep the carboy at ambient temperature in the range 64°F–72°F (18°C–22°C). MLF can take as little as a couple of weeks, or perhaps months, depending on temperature, wine pH and other factors.*

☐ **6.1** Dissolve 1 tsp malolactic nutrients in a little lukewarm water, add to the carboy, mix thoroughly but gently.

☐ **6.2** Gently stir in one packet of your choice of liquid malolactic culture, 125 mL of Wyeast 4007 or 35 mL of White Labs WLP675. Stir thoroughly until well dispersed, then place the airlock and bung back on.

☐ **6.3** Once a week, gently stir the lees into suspension to favor a good MLF. Be sure to stir *very gently* to avoid oxygen uptake. During

MLF, you may be able to see tiny bubbles slowly rising to the surface if you shine a flashlight at the top of the carboy.

☐ **6.4**   When bubbles have subsided completely, run a paper chromatography test. If in doubt and you cannot see bubbles during the MLF, run a test every 2 weeks. MLF is complete if the malic spot has completely disappeared. If not complete, go back to Step 6.3. If you cannot get the MLF to complete within 2 months, you'll need to treat the wine with lysozyme as described in the section RESIDUAL MALIC ACID in Chapter NINE.

☐ **6.5**   When the MLF is complete, transfer the carboy to a cool cellar, take a sample, measure and record TA and pH to assess the impact of MLF. TA should be lower and pH higher than the measurements taken in Step 5.2.

☐ **6.6**   Dissolve ¼ tsp KMS or 4 crushed Campden tablets in cool water, and gently stir into the wine. Secure the carboy with an airlock and bung and allow to age.

Store the wine as cool as possible to around 55°F (13°C) from here on. Try not to exceed 68°F (20°C), which could otherwise shorten the life of the wine.

STEP 7 – AGING

☐ **7.1**   Sanitize the oak infusion tube, drop 1 cup of medium-toast (MT) oak chips in it and secure both ends. Insert the loaded infusion tube into the carboy, and secure the carboy with an airlock and bung.

You can simply remove the infusion tube and oak chips when the wine is oaked to your liking; this saves you a racking. If you simply drop the chips into the carboy, you'll need to rack the wine, and that can become a nuisance with chips blocking the racking cane.

Alternatively, if you want to infuse oak and age the wine slower and longer, use one (1) MT oak stick. You don't need the infusion tube; simply attach the stick to the bung using a short length of fishing line and a stainless steel screw.

Every couple of weeks, smell and taste the wine to see how the infusion is progressing—you don't want to overdo it. The wine may be ready in as little as one month if using chips depending on the kind of chips.

☐ **7.2** Add sulfite every 3 months during aging; dissolve ⅛ tsp KMS or 2 crushed Campden tablets in cool water, and gently stir into the wine.

☐ **7.3** Pull the infusion tube or oak stick out when the wine is oaked to your liking. You can age the wine some more for 12–18 months, even more if you wish. Taste the wine each time you add sulfite to determine when you feel the wine is ready to be bottled.

STEP 8 – CLARIFICATION AND STABILIZATION

ⓘ *Be sure to place the airlock and bung back on the carboy after each step.*

☐ **8.1** When the wine is to your liking, rack to a sanitized carboy. Assess the clarity, and if sufficiently clear, proceed to STEP 9 – FILTERING, or STEP 10 – BOTTLING if you want to skip filtering too.

☐ **8.2** If you want to clarify the wine further, add the packet of Kieselsol suspension while stirring continuously for about 2 minutes.

☐ **8.3** The next day, add the packet of chitosan and stir thoroughly for about 2 minutes.

☐ **8.4** Let the wine stand until completely clear, then rack to a sanitized carboy.

STEP 9 – FILTERING (OPTIONAL)

ⓘ *Filtering is only required if the wine shows any slight haze or if you want a crystal clear appearance.*

☐ **9.1** Clean and sanitize all filtering equipment, including hoses, and pads or cartridges.

☐ **9.2** First filter with no. 1 or AF1/AF2 pads or a 10-micron cartridge into another carboy. Rinse the first carboy.

Do not be tempted to skip this first step to save on filtering—you'll be pulling your hair out.

9.3 Filter with no. 2 or AF3 pads or a 5-micron cartridge back into the first carboy. Rinse the other carboy.

 This second filtering is often sufficient, but you can proceed with step 9.4 and the third filtering, if desired.

9.4 Filter with no. 3 or AF4 pads or a 1-micron cartridge into the other carboy.

9.5 You'll likely have "lost" about half a bottle's worth of wine, and so, top up accordingly, and place the airlock and bung back on the carboy.

STEP 10 – BOTTLING

10.1 When ready to bottle, first dissolve ¼ tsp KMS or 4 crushed Campden tablets in cool water, and gently stir into the wine, and then proceed with bottling.

10.2 Clean and sanitize bottles and all bottling equipment.

10.3 Fill bottles, cork each bottle as soon as filled, and apply capsules and labels.

10.4 Store bottles right side up for a few days, then store horizontally in a cool cellar.

 Wait at least 1 week, perhaps more, especially if you have filtered the wine, to allow the wine to settle and get over bottle shock so that it tastes as it did before bottling.

10.5 You can bottle age some more as the wine will slowly improve over the next few months.

10.6 Enjoy!

CHAPTER SEVENTEEN

Dealing with Problems

*A*ll winemakers, aspiring and seasoned ones alike, will have to deal with a problem wine, flawed or spoiled, at some point. It happens!

Your approach to fixing a problem will depend on how soon you realize the wine has a flaw or fault, identifying the exact nature of the defect, including possible root causes and solutions, how quickly you take action to remedy the problem, and if the wine is even salvageable.

This chapter describes how to go about identifying and fixing some of the most common wine defects, complex ones too, and how to avoid them in the first place.

It's not always easy or straightforward. Call upon an experienced winemaking friend if you can't pinpoint the problem or root cause and ask for advice or guidance, or consult ModernHomeWinemaking.com for additional information and more advanced tips. If the wine is beyond repair, don't be tempted to blend it with a perfectly sound wine—the result will be an inferior wine. It definitely hurts to have to dump the wine down the drain after investing so much time and money, but it can be unhealthy to stubbornly drink it anyway.

MY WINE HAS TURNED A BROWNISH COLOR

Oxidation is by far the most common winemaking problem. It manifests itself in different ways and to different extents, but the first visual cue of a problem is the color turning darker, progressively toward brown.

What Causes the Problem

All wines oxidize—and at a rate based on the type of wine and storage conditions. But when wine is exposed to oxygen and remains unprotected, it will soon turn darkish. White wines are significantly more fragile and more susceptible to oxidation and will turn a progressively browner color, similar to sherry (a Spanish fortified wine which is purposely allowed to oxidize), whereas reds will first take on orange hues and then progressively turn browner.

Oxygen and oxidation are the culprits. Oxidation causes certain "good" wine compounds to oxidize and transform into "bad" compounds that can affect color, aromas, flavors, and overall quality. Common causes of oxidation include:

- Too much headspace
- Excessive exposure to air during processing
- Insufficient sulfite, sulfur dioxide (SO_2)
- A defective or poor airlock/bung while wine is still in carboys, or a defective or poor cork if it's in bottles
- High storage temperature
- Storage in oxygen-permeable carboys, such as the blue ones for bottled water that are made from polycarbonate plastic instead of PET.

Oxidation can happen in juice, too, when it is overly exposed to oxygen, although in such a case, it is caused by enzymes that can be easily inhibited with sulfite.

How to Assess the Problem

First determine if the oxidation is limited to browning, as it can also cause other problems such as acetic acid and volatile acidity (VA), ethyl acetate, and acetaldehyde, if not halted. These are described below.

Pour some wine in a glass, hold it up against a source of light, and evaluate the color. Then swirl the glass, smell the wine, and repeat a couple of times. Take a sip and taste, and repeat.

If the wine smells and tastes good and it's just a matter of color, then you've detected the problem early and you'll be able to fix it. From the list above, identify the root cause.

How to Fix

You have to act quickly—as soon as you identify the problem and root cause—to limit further damage if the wine is still in carboys.

If a white wine is uncharacteristically turning amber but is not giving off any foul aromas or flavors, add sulfite immediately. Dissolve ½ tsp potassium metabisulfite or 8 crushed Campden tablets in 100 mL of cool water and stir into the carboy. Then treat with casein, followed by PVPP, making sure to top up the carboy. Rack when completely settled and clear and bottle as soon as possible. Consume the wine without aging—it will likely not improve.

If a red wine is turning orange or has some browning but no foul aromas or flavors, simply add sulfite at the same rate, bottle, and consume.

How to Prevent

Implement and follow sound winemaking practices to prevent oxidation:
- Avoid excessive exposure to air during processing
- Process wine as gently as possible
- Top up carboys
- Use sulfite and add regularly as recommended
- Verify the integrity of all equipment, particularly airlocks and bungs
- Use good-quality no. 9 corks for bottling
- Store wine in a cool cellar or area, ideally around 55°F (13°C)
- Invest in the necessary equipment to measure free SO_2 and become familiar with managing and adjusting free SO_2.

MY WINE SMELLS LIKE VINEGAR

Vinegar is acetic acid, which yeast produces in tiny amounts that contribute to a wine's aromas and flavors. This means that acetic acid is always present in wine, but if you can smell it, this points to a problem, possibly another type of oxidation problem known as volatile acidity, or VA.

Inexperienced tasters and novice winemakers often do not recognize VA. We also all have different detection thresholds, so sometimes you won't detect it early. As VA increases, it can reach a point where the wine becomes spoiled and is best discarded.

What Causes the Problem

Acetic acid and VA are the result of the oxidation of ethanol (the alcohol in wine) by acetic acid bacteria (known as *Acetobacter*), which thrive in the presence of oxygen. This can happen when you have too much headspace in carboys or there is some piece of defective equipment, such as a bad airlock or bung, while there is not enough SO_2 protecting the wine. It's a very common problem in poorly managed wines aging in barrels. Fruit flies, too, are a problem. They are carriers of *Acetobacter*, so you have to keep them out of your winemaking area.

How to Assess the Problem

First determine if the problem is limited to acetic acid (evidenced by a vinegar smell) and VA. As you cannot measure VA without proper lab equipment, you need to rely on your ability to smell and detect it. If you detect a bruised-apple kind of smell (due to acetaldehyde; see below), you have an imminent VA problem that you can now prevent or at least limit its damage. In more advanced spoilage cases, wine can smell of nail polish remover (due to ethyl acetate; see below).

How to Fix

You can't remove VA from wine, not at home-winemaking scale.

If there is only a hint of VA, the wine is likely still drinkable. Add sulfite immediately; dissolve ½ tsp potassium metabisulfite or 8 crushed Campden tablets in 100 mL of cool water and stir into the carboy. Top up the carboy. Bottle as soon as possible and consume without aging.

If there is a strong smell of VA, there is no remedy, and it is best to dump the wine. Never blend it into a perfectly sound wine; the result will be an inferior wine.

How to Prevent

Implement and follow the sound winemaking practices described above in the section MY WINE HAS TURNED A BROWNISH COLOR to prevent oxidation.

And remember—since bacteria thrive at higher pH values (greater than 3.65), you need to add more SO_2. Double the recommended amount on the first addition (½ tsp potassium metabisulfite or 8 crushed Campden tablets) when fermentation is complete.

If you have had a VA problem, your cellar is infected with *Acetobacter*, putting all your winemaking at higher risk. Assume that *Acetobacter* are always present, just waiting for the right conditions to strike, so don't give them a fighting chance. Implement strict hygiene measures and maintain proper SO_2 levels in wine. Do your best to keep fruit flies away from your winemaking area; place a lid or tarp while fermenting in a pail or vat.

MY WINE SMELLS LIKE BRUISED, ROTTEN APPLES

The smell of bruised or rotten apples is the result of a pungent substance called acetaldehyde, which is also something yeast produces during fermentation in tiny, undetectable amounts that contribute to aroma complexity as well as color stability in rosés and reds. However, when acetaldehyde is excessive and detectable, this points to an oxidation problem. Moreover, acetaldehyde increases the perception of alcohol, making wine taste overly strong.

What Causes the Problem

Acetaldehyde is the result of ethanol oxidation from causes similar to those that produce acetic acid and VA. Given its low detection threshold and that it is a precursor to VA, if you smell acetaldehyde, you have an imminent VA problem.

How to Assess the Problem

Acetaldehyde has a very low detection threshold and a distinct bruised- or rotten-apple smell. You can detect it easily and hopefully early, before the onset of VA. You can usually pick up the smell when you open a carboy, but you can also pour a sample into a glass to smell and confirm. Act quickly as you have limited time to solve this problem.

How to Fix

Acetaldehyde binds very strongly with sulfite, and once bound, it becomes non-volatile, meaning you can no longer smell it. As soon as you detect any hint of acetaldehyde, add sulfite immediately. Dissolve ¼ tsp potassium metabisulfite or 4 crushed Campden tablets in 100 mL of cool water and stir into the carboy, then taste the wine again. If you still smell acetaldehyde, add another similar dose of sulfite and taste again. Repeat one last time if needed, after which, if the smell persists, the wine is likely beyond fixing and is best discarded.

How to Prevent

Implement and follow the sound winemaking practices described above in the section MY WINE HAS TURNED A BROWNISH COLOR to prevent oxidation.

MY WINE SMELLS LIKE NAIL POLISH REMOVER

The smell of nail polish remover is the result of a substance called ethyl acetate, and it's very nasty in wine. It's another common oxidation problem that follows VA.

What Causes the Problem

Ethyl acetate occurs due to the esterification of excessive amounts of acetic acid, resulting from causes similar to those that produce VA. Esterification is a chemical reaction between alcohol and an acid—ethanol and acetic acid here—that forms an ester, a volatile substance.

How to Assess the Problem

As you cannot measure ethyl acetate without very advanced analytical equipment and expertise, here too, you have to rely on your ability to smell and detect it. You might even get a hot sensation on the tongue, and if you do, the wine is likely beyond salvage.

How to Fix

You won't be able to fix this problem; it's a really tough one. It's best to discard the wine.

How to Prevent

Implement and follow the sound winemaking practices described above in the sections MY WINE HAS TURNED A BROWNISH COLOR and MY WINE SMELLS OF VINEGAR to prevent oxidation.

THERE'S A WHITE FILM ON THE SURFACE OF MY WINE

This is another oxidation-related problem: a whitish film floating and expanding on the surface of wine. It is often referred to as mycoderma, named after the culprit aerobic surface yeast *Candida mycoderma*.

What Causes the Problem

Aerobic surface yeast thrives on oxygen in poorly topped-up, neglected carboys (or any vessel, especially barrels). It starts off by forming a small floating patch that grows and is able to do so even in the presence of SO_2.

How to Assess the Problem

If you have any headspace in your carboy and you notice surface film, the cause is straightforward. It is more disconcerting when you discover it in a fully topped carboy after months of aging and under the protection of SO_2. First inspect the airlock and bung; you likely have a poor seal, possibly from a fractured seam in the airlock, or perhaps the airlock has run dry.

If you notice surface film, assess for other oxidation problems described above. If there are no other problems and you feel the wine can be salvaged, you can try to fix it.

How to Fix

If the wine reaches into the neck of the carboy, remove as much surface film as possible by flooding the carboy with a similar wine until the film overflows out. Either pour wine gently down the wall of the carboy or feed from a hose inserted well below the surface. The idea is to disturb the film as little as possible as it breaks up very easily, and then it becomes difficult to remove. Wrap the top of the carboy with paper towels to avoid making a mess.

SURFACE FILM

SPOILED VOLUME TO DISCARD

VOLUME TO RACK

Figure 17.1: Dealing with surface film and spoiled wine.

If there is a large headspace with the wine level low in the carboy, for example, below the shoulder (Figure 17.1), the flooding method will not work as you would disturb the film and it would fall into the wine. A considerable amount of wine would also be required to flood the film out. Instead, using a wine thief or kitchen baster, draw a sample of wine from just below the surface, then taste. If the wine does not taste good, draw another sample from lower under the surface, and taste. Repeat this process until you have reached a level where the wine is good. Then rack the volume of good wine to another carboy; the idea is to leave the volume of spoiled wine behind.

Add sulfite—dissolve ¼ tsp potassium metabisulfite or 4 crushed Campden tablets in 100 mL of cool water, and stir into the carboy. Top up and place the airlock and bung back on.

How to Prevent

Implement and follow the sound winemaking practices described above in the sections MY WINE HAS TURNED A BROWNISH COLOR and MY WINE SMELLS OF VINEGAR to prevent oxidation.

MY WINE SMELLS LIKE ROTTEN EGGS, A SEWER

Odors of rotten eggs, sewer, cooked cabbage, struck flint, or burnt rubber are the result of a substance known as hydrogen sulfide, often simply referred to as sulfide or H_2S, which can be detected at very low levels, in the parts-per-billion range.

Some winemakers will also refer to this condition as "reduction" and declare a wine as having a reductive character. Reduction is the opposite of oxidation. A substance becomes oxidized in the presence of oxygen, whereas a substance may become reduced in the absence of oxygen, and that's how hydrogen sulfide forms.

What Causes the Problem

There are many possible causes of H_2S in wine, the most common being wine left on the thick layer of gross lees for too long at the end of fermentation and not racked sufficiently quickly. Gross lees undergo yeast autolysis—that is, dead yeast cells in the lees break down, decompose, and then, in the absence of oxygen, start producing H_2S.

Another common cause is stressed fermentation. Undue stress on yeast can be caused by insufficient or excessive nutrients or too cold or too hot of a fermentation.

Yeast also produces H_2S as part of its metabolism, and different strains produce different amounts. Any substance with a sulfur component in juice may cause yeast to generate larger amounts of H_2S. For example, elemental sulfur from the overuse of sulfur-based vineyard sprays or fungicides to control mildew or a harvest too close to spraying will cause fermentation to produce more H_2S. Reds will tend to develop H_2S more commonly due to elemental sulfur, given that grape solids are macerated in the juice and wine.

If H_2S is left untreated, it can react with alcohol and produce other unpleasant odors of raw onions, rubber, natural gas, or skunk, all of which can be very difficult, if not impossible, to remove.

How to Assess the Problem

H_2S-related odors are easy to detect. You'll usually smell H_2S as soon as you open a carboy or uncover a vat for a punchdown. If you do suspect a problem, pour a sample in a tasting glass to confirm.

How to Fix

If you detect a mild case of H_2S in red wine during fermentation, agitate the wine by stirring vigorously to dissipate the smell and add another dose of complex yeast nutrients. You can substitute diammonium phosphate (DAP) for the complex nutrients. The condition should clear up within a day or two. If the wine is in a carboy, try splash racking vigorously into another carboy and repeat once more if necessary. If the smell persists, you have a more serious case of H_2S that will require a different treatment. The splash racking technique is not recommended for whites and rosés as it may cause oxidation problems.

For whites, rosés, and excessive H_2S in reds, winemakers use a 1% solution of copper sulfate ($CuSO_4$) because it is very effective, but this requires some know-how and experience, as excessive use can leave toxic and harmful amounts of copper behind. If you are comfortable working with copper sulfate, consult *Modern Home Winemaking* or ModernHome Winemaking.com to learn how to conduct bench trials with copper sulfate and to treat a batch of wine.

You'll also probably read on the internet about running wine through copper piping or dropping some old (pre-1982) pennies into a carboy.

Yes, these can remove H_2S, but they can leave harmful amounts of copper behind, and so these practices are discouraged.

Your best bet is to seek out a couple of copper-based but safer products that use inactivated yeast, either Reduless or Kupzit. You'll have to research and find where these are sold in small packs. Follow product instructions very carefully. Add the lowest amount recommended and repeat it if the odor persists, but never exceed the maximum. If the maximum amount of Reduless or Kupzit does not fix the problem, then no safe amount will work. Rack the wine after 3 days, followed by coarse and medium filtrations.

How to Prevent

You can prevent H_2S by implementing the following best practices:

- Don't harvest too close to vineyard spraying if you grow your own grapes
- Add complex nutrients to juice/must when launching fermentation and then again when SG has dropped by one-third
- Avoid yeast strains that produce large amounts of H_2S, or consider using a so-called "H_2S-preventing" yeast
- Avoid stressing yeast by ameliorating high-SG juice and fermenting at recommended temperatures
- Go easy with sulfite at crush or when cold settling juice
- Aerate reds during fermentation and rack wine off the gross lees within 2 days of completion.

MY WINE HAS STOPPED FERMENTING

See the section WHAT IF FERMENTATION STOPS BEFORE IT COMPLETES? in Chapter SIX.

MY MLF DOESN'T SEEM TO BE PROGRESSING

See the section WHAT IF I CAN'T GET MLF TO COMPLETE? in Chapter SEVEN.

MY RED WINE TURNED OUT TOO LIGHT, NOT AS DARK AS IT SHOULD

Color is the first visual cue we use to form our first impression of a red (or rosé) wine, and even if the wine smells and tastes wonderful, a lighter than desirable color may cause us to misjudge its quality.

What Causes the Problem

Red wines derive their color from anthocyanins, the color pigment substances extracted from skins during maceration and fermentation. (Teinturiers also derive their color from anthocyanins in the pulp.) A light color can result from under-extraction, or the variety or the quality of the vintage are such that grapes have less anthocyanins to offer no matter how long you macerate. Wine pH is also a factor—the higher the pH, the less the color and intensity.

There is also a substantial loss of color during fermentation, as well as during aging, but much less so. Some color loss is expected as anthocyanins react with other substances and drop out; however, there can be significant losses if you don't proactively stabilize color during fermentation and aging. Color loss can also be due to an anthocyanin–tannin imbalance; that is, a richly colored wine with too few tannins will soon shed substantial color (see the section MY WINE LACKS BODY, IT'S TOO LIGHT below). Excessive use of sulfite can also bleach color.

How to Assess the Problem

First look back at your winemaking process and notes to zero in on the likely culprit from the list of possible causes.

Taste the wine to assess its tannin profile. If the wine is richly colored but tastes unusually light and lacks body (due to low tannins), then the wine has an anthocyanin–tannin imbalance and is at risk of shedding more color during aging.

How to Fix

To restore some of the red color and intensity, run some trials: add tartaric acid to lower pH, provided that the style of wine allows for more acidity, or add tannins to stabilize anthocyanins and slow down color loss. You could also blend the wine with a richly colored one, if available; adding a touch of Alicante Bouschet, Petite Sirah or Norton, for example, can do wonders to a light red.

How to Prevent

At crush, add oak powder or grape tannins to help stabilize color, particularly when working with varieties known to pose a challenge while extracting and preserving color. Use enzymes to help with color extraction, and ferment at warmer temperatures in the range 77°F–86°F (25°C–30°C). Increase the frequency and "aggressiveness" of punchdowns, and be patient—don't rush through fermentation. Finally, add more tannins during aging to stabilize color.

Here's a great technique that will do wonders for color: transfer crushed, destemmed grapes and juice to a pail and secure it shut with a lid. Place the pail in a deep freezer until well frozen, then remove, let thaw, and ferment as usual. The freezing–thawing cycle causes grape-skin cell walls to rupture to a greater extent and release more color.

For rosés, extract more color than your desired final color, knowing that there will be substantial loss. You can also run off, say, 10% of the juice after crushing to increase the skin-to-juice ratio and color. Simply ferment the run-off juice separately as a white wine. You can do that with a red wine too—why not?

Consider adding pasteurized, crushed, and destemmed grapes, such as Allgrape Pack, when making small volumes from lightly colored juice.

Finally, don't use more sulfite than necessary in order to avoid bleaching color.

MY REDS TASTE TOO ASTRINGENT, TOO BITTER

Astringency and bitterness are often used interchangeably, and although both involve tannins, they mean different things.

Astringency is a tactile sensation of dryness and roughness on the palate caused by wine tannins binding with saliva proteins when you taste and drink red wine. Bitterness describes the bitter taste of some kinds of tannins.

What Causes the Problem

There are many, many kinds of tannins in red wine with very different tactile, taste, and chemical characteristics. We'll keep it simple here and refer to "good tannins" as those extracted from red grape skins and which are desirable in wine, and "bad tannins," sometimes called "green tannins," as those extracted from seeds and stems and which are undesirable.

Astringency occurs due to the presence of excessive amounts of good tannins from over-extraction during maceration and fermentation or from overuse of oak. As tannins interact with other tannins and other red wine substances during aging, they become "softer," and astringency diminishes. This makes the wine feel less dry, less rough on the palate.

Bitterness occurs due to the extraction of bad tannins when seeds are carelessly fractured during punchdowns or when excessive stems, especially very green or crushed stems, are left to macerate with the wine.

How to Assess the Problem

First determine whether you are dealing with astringency or bitterness—dry/rough sensation as opposed to bitter taste—and then identify possible causes in your winemaking. Also look at your TA (total acidity) numbers to make sure that acidity is not a factor, as high acidity will make tannins taste harsher.

How to Fix

If your wine is too bitter or too astringent and you don't want to wait for years for tannins to soften or mellow, treat the batch with gelatin or PVPP. If TA is high, and assuming the wine has gone through MLF, try a small deacidification of no more than 1 g/L TA with potassium bicarbonate, or perhaps cold crash the wine to drop some tartaric acid.

How to Prevent

Learn the tannin characteristics of whatever grape variety you'll be processing. Different grapes have different kinds and amounts of tannins. Likewise for proteins, which can impact tannin transfer into wine. Macerate and ferment accordingly—that is, if you are partial to less tannic wines but you are working with a high-tannin variety, consider limiting maceration during fermentation and press earlier.

Remove as many stems as possible, as those contribute harsh, bitter tannins, and be careful not to damage seeds at the bottom of your pail or vat when doing punchdowns.

MY WINE LACKS BODY, IT'S TOO LIGHT

Body goes hand in hand with balance—that is, balance among alcohol, acidity, sweetness, and tannins in the case of reds and some whites like, for example, oak-aged Chardonnay.

What Causes the Problem

Wine drinkers often describe wine as being light, thin, lacking body, and just based on low alcohol. This is not necessarily always the case. A low-alcohol wine, say 11% ABV, can taste full bodied, whereas a higher-alcohol wine like, for example, 13% ABV can taste light and lacking body. Tannins are a big part of body.

How to Assess the Problem

If a wine tastes light, too light for its style or your palate, first look at the data in your notes. Look at % ABV from the initial PA (Potential Alcohol), TA, final SG or how much sweetening agent you added and assess tannins based on taste impressions. Which of these stands out as a likely cause of imbalance?

How to Fix

If after evaluation you determine that the wine lacks body or is thin because it has low alcohol, consider blending it with another higher-alcohol wine in whatever proportions that please your palate. Run some simple trials to see what works best for you.

If the cause is low acidity, low sweetness, or low tannins, try increasing whichever is too low, being mindful of their opposing effects, or, here too, consider blending if you have a suitable wine available. You can also add tartaric acid to increase acidity, table sugar for sweetness, and grape tannins or oak powder to get more tannins.

Also try adding some glycerin or, better yet, some gum arabic to increase mouthfeel—that is, to give a feeling of fullness, or more volume, in the mouth. Gum arabic is usually sold as a ready-to-use solution with a concentration of 20% or 30%. Add 20–30 mL of gum arabic per carboy of ready-to-bottle wine. Do not add it to wine intended for long aging, as it can interfere with tannin–anthocyanin reactions and cause undesirable effects. If you are filtering your wine, do not add gum arabic until after the final filtration, as it may clog filters.

How to Prevent

Always measure SG and TA *before* fermentation, adjust if needed, and taste the wine during fermentation to determine how long to macerate and when to proceed to pressing, to make sure you are extracting sufficient tannins from grape skins, particularly in light-skinned varieties.

MY WINE TASTES SOUR

Sourness occurs due to acidity, one of the main pillars of wine balance (the others being alcohol, sweetness, and tannins). Acidity adds freshness, but if excessive, it will make the wine taste overly sour and not enjoyable. It can also make tannins taste overly harsh.

What Causes the Problem

The usual culprit is high acidity—that is, TA—due to high amounts of tartaric acid or malic acid or both. This is assuming that the wine is not affected by VA, which is a whole different problem (see the section MY WINE SMELLS OF VINEGAR above).

A wine can also taste sour at normal acidity levels if there are excessive tannins. This is why whites, which essentially have no tannins, have higher acidity than reds. It's also the reason why reds are not served chilled; colder temperatures increase the perception of acidity, which would make tannins taste harsher.

It could also be that your palate prefers wines that are not too dry—that is, wines with some residual sugars and a little sweetness that offset some of the acidity.

How to Assess the Problem

First re-measure TA (and pH) to understand where your acidity level is at, then determine from your winemaking records when and why it became too high. Did acidity go up after fermentation? Did it not go down from MLF? Or perhaps TA is okay and you're just finding the wine too dry. Maybe you've over-extracted tannins in that bold red you made. Also, make sure you degassed the wine properly; excessive residual gas makes wine taste more acidic.

How to Fix

Whenever acidity is too high once wine has finished fermenting, it's never a good idea to deacidify, at least not by any significant amounts. There is a great likelihood that you'll exacerbate the imbalance, over-process the wine, and create faults. A small deacidification not exceeding 1 g/L is okay, and if MLF is desired, then proceed with the MLF—that will lower acidity, possibly significantly if there is a lot of malic acid to convert.

Alternatively, if acidity is within the ideal range but you find the wine too dry, you can sweeten it to offset some of the acidity. Run bench trials first to determine how much sugar to add, then treat the rest of the batch (see the section SWEETENING: BALANCING ACIDITY AND SWEET-NESS in Chapter TEN). Stabilize the wine with sulfite and sorbate (only if the wine has not gone through MLF).

Degas the wine if this was not previously done. If the wine was not cold stabilized, try cold crashing (see the section TARTRATES in Chapter NINE) to drop some of the tartaric acid to lower acidity.

How to Prevent

Measure TA in the juice and make any adjustments *before* fermentation. Limit tannin extraction in high-acid red varietals, such as Barbera, Nebbiolo, Marquette, and Norton.

MY WINE IS TOO SWEET

Sweetness plays an important role in whites and rosés in balancing acidity, but if excessive, it will make the wine taste overly sweet and not enjoyable.

What Causes the Problem

The usual culprit is high amounts of residual sugars from an unfinished fermentation. There can be significant amounts of unfermented sugars when the final SG is above 0.995. If the wine seems too sweet but it was fermented completely dry, then acidity is likely too low.

How to Assess the Problem

First make sure that you are tasting and assessing the wine at the "right" temperature. Whites are served chilled, which increases the perception of acidity, while for the opposite reason, reds are served at ambient temperatures so that the acidity does not clash with tannins. Then re-measure SG and TA so that you can work out possible solutions.

How to Fix

If fermentation is not complete—that is, SG is not at or below 0.995—try and complete it, if possible. Be forewarned! If it has stalled, it may be very difficult to get it to restart, especially if the SG is low. If you can't get fermentation to restart and complete to dryness, try acidifying with tartaric acid. Before treating a whole batch, run bench trials to determine how much acid to add to balance the sweetness. Remember to stabilize with sulfite and sorbate (only if the wine has not gone through MLF).

How to Prevent

It's always best to ferment wine to complete dryness and then sweeten to taste when sweetness is desired. Trying to stop an active fermentation at some desired sweet spot is quite a challenge.

MY WINE IS FIZZY, ALMOST LIKE SPARKLING WINE

This specifically refers to a previously still wine—that is, a wine that had been adequately degassed and had no perceptible fizz on the palate at bottling—which now tastes slightly fizzy or even carbonated. There may be visible sediment, often mistaken for tartrates by those not familiar with tartrates—the latter are crystals, not powder-like. In the worst case, corks pop or bottles explode from pressure build-up.

What Causes the Problem

Assuming that the wine was properly degassed, this problem occurs due to refermentation in bottles. This happens when wine did not ferment to complete dryness and was not properly stabilized. This is a common occurrence in sweetened wines or with novice winemakers rushing to bottle but not understanding the implications of residual sugars and incomplete or improper stabilization.

How to Assess the Problem

Do a visual inspection and taste the wine. If you suspect that it has started refermenting in bottles, look for any *fine* sediment—the fine lees that form during fermentation—making sure not to confuse these with tartrates, which are bigger and shinier, having a crystal-like appearance. Hold the bottle by the neck and turn it upside down; if the lees make the wine cloudy, it is a sure sign of refermentation. Uncork the bottle and taste the wine; if it tastes fizzy, it is definitely a refermentation problem.

How to Fix

If it's a refermentation problem, you have no choice but to uncork all the bottles and to pour the wine back into a carboy. Let the wine ferment to complete dryness—i.e., an SG of 0.995 or lower—rack, and finally stabilize with sulfite and sorbate (if the wine had not undergone MLF). You can then safely rebottle.

If it's a case of insufficient degassing, you can simply drink the wine as is, or uncork all bottles and pour the wine back into a carboy, degas, and rebottle.

How to Prevent

To avoid refermentation problems, always ferment to dryness with an SG of 0.995 or lower, and stabilize with sulfite and also sorbate as a precaution, again, if the wine had not undergone any MLF.

MY WINE WAS CLEAR, NOW IT'S CLOUDY AND NOT CLEARING

A perfectly clear wine can unexpectedly become cloudy or fail to clear in spite of clarification treatments.

What Causes the Problem

Persistent cloudiness or clarification problems in wines can occur due to pectin, but in whites and rosés, these problems are most likely the result

of proteins. For more information, refer to the sections PECTIN and PRO-
TEINS, respectively, in Chapter NINE.

How to Assess the Problem

If you have a cloudy white or rosé wine that had previously cleared, it's a
protein problem. But if you have a cloudy wine that had never properly
cleared, it can be a pectin issue. This is particularly true of wines from
high-pectin Native American varieties or hybrids, or of fruit or country
wines. It could be a protein issue in non-red wines. *V. labrusca* varieties
tend to be high in pectin, Concord notoriously so.

How to Fix

If you suspect a pectin problem, add pectic enzymes, let settle, then rack
and filter. If in doubt, try a pectic enzyme treatment before treating for
proteins. If you suspect a protein problem, treat with bentonite or silica–
gel (e.g., Kieselsol/gelatin), let settle, then rack and filter.

How to Prevent

To prevent pectin problems when working with varieties or fruit known
to contain large amounts of pectin, treat the juice/must with higher doses
of pectic enzymes. To prevent a protein haze, treat the juice/must with
bentonite or silica–gel.

I SEE TINY SHARDS OF GLASS IN BOTTLES

What you see are tartrate crystals, or simply tartrates. They are often referred to as wine diamonds. Although many winemakers and wine con-
noisseurs find them completely acceptable (some even suggest they are a
sign of good winemaking), to the beginners, tartrates at the bottom of
bottles or stuck to wine corks may indeed seem like a cause for concern
as they look like tiny shards of glass, but they are harmless.

What Causes the Problem

Tartrates are the result of wine having been subjected to cold temperatures. Their presence indicates incomplete or lack of cold stabilization.
For more information, refer to the section TARTRATES in Chapter NINE.

How to Assess the Problem

Tartrates are often mistaken for other kinds of sediment. They form crystals, perhaps powder-thin ones, but if you flip a bottle upside down, the crystals simply float down and precipitate, whereas other forms of sediment, like those from refermentation, remain suspended and give wine a cloudy appearance.

How to Fix

If the wine is already bottled, it's best to leave it alone. It's not worth the trouble of uncorking all the bottles, pouring the wine back into a carboy, and rebottling. Just be careful pouring wine when serving. If you notice tartrates in a carboy, rack the wine before bottling, but give it extra time to make sure that crystallization has indeed completed after a cold stabilization treatment. Crystals continue to form ever so slowly after treatment and are not always immediately visible.

How to Prevent

To stabilize against tartrates, you can cold crash the wine or, alternatively, if you can source such products, add a tartrate inhibitor, such as carboxymethyl cellulose (CMC) or potassium polyaspartate.

MY RED WINE STAINS BOTTLES

In reds, some narrow glass staining along the length of horizontally stored bottles is acceptable, but not when it's excessive, not when the entire glass is stained all around. It's also a pain to wash bottles, and you'll possibly need to use an alkaline cleaner to remove stains if you reuse bottles.

What Causes the Problem

Excessive glass staining means you bottled much too soon, likely with no fining or filtering, just relying on natural sedimentation to clarify wine. But ah! You'll say that filtering removes color. Filtering removes what eventually sediments or stains glass. And it can still happen with richly colored, tannic reds that have aged for 12 months, even 18–24 months, and which you have racked multiple times. Tannins and anthocyanins, those color pigment molecules, continuously bind and precipitate to form a very thin layer of sediment that can stick to glass like super glue. From a clarification point of view, multiple rackings offer no advantage compared to a single racking done at the end of the same time frame.

How to Assess the Problem

If you bottled red wine within 12 months with no fining or filtering, expect considerable staining. The richer the wine, the more staining you can expect. If you fined, then it likely was not sufficient for that type of wine. And if you did filter, regardless of any fining, you likely used pads or cartridge with too high a rating without filtering down using "tighter" filter pads or cartridges.

How to Fix

There is no sense in emptying bottles into a carboy and reprocessing the wine. The amount of work and the exposure of wine to oxygen do not warrant reprocessing. And if you notice staining in a carboy and you want to bottle soon, then you have to take preventive action.

How to Prevent

You have several options depending on how soon you want to bottle, how quickly you expect to consume the wine, and whether you want to fine or filter or do both. If you prefer not to filter and if you'll be drinking the wine relatively quickly, you can add gum arabic to ready-to-bottle wine just before bottling (see the section MY WINE LACKS BODY, IT'S TOO LIGHT above).

A better way to prevent heavy sedimentation or any serious glass staining is to bulk age red wine for a minimum of 18 months. Remember that red wine continues to improve as it ages, so there is no sense in rushing to bottle and drink. When done aging, carefully rack into another carboy, then, assuming that the wine has cleared well on its own, filter with coarse pads (e.g., Buon Vino no. 1 pads or AF2 round pads) or a 5-micron cartridge and again with polishing pads (e.g., Buon Vino no. 2 pads or AF3 round pads) or a 1-micron cartridge.

MY WINE SMELLS OF GREEN BELL PEPPERS

When unappealing vegetal-like aromas—green bell pepper and freshly cut grass—dominate in red wine, they distract from the enjoyment and are considered a flaw.

What Causes the Problem

The smells are the result of substances known as pyrazines, which occur naturally in red Cabernet-related varieties—Cabernet Franc, Cabernet Sauvignon, Merlot, and Carménère—as well as Malbec but slowly disappear as grapes ripen. However, pyrazines and their telltale smell will persist into wine if the grapes have been harvested too early or if they have weathered a colder-than-usual growing season. You'll often pick up hints of green bell peppers in Cabernet-based wines made from fruit grown in cool climates.

How to Assess the Problem

This flaw is easily detected: the wine has an unmistakable smell of green bell peppers and freshly cut grass.

How to Fix

This is a tough one to fix; pyrazines can't be removed, and the only recourse is masking the offending odors. Oak can do wonders here. Untoasted oak can mask the vegetal character in wine by intensifying the fruity expression and bringing forward "ripe" fruit notes without the aromas of toasted oak.

To treat a carboy, add 1 cup of untoasted or lightly toasted oak chips. Taste, smell, and assess the wine once a week. Remove the chips (if held in an infusion tube) or rack the wine when the odors are sufficiently masked. If successful, add up to 4 tsp of tannins to further improve aromas and flavors. Start with 1 tsp, taste and assess, and repeat until you hit your sweet spot, but don't exceed 4 tsp.

How to Prevent

If you suspect that your pyrazine-prone grapes were harvested prematurely (an unusually low SG is a good indicator) or sourced from a cool or cold-climate grape-growing region, in addition to ½ cup of oak powder added at crush for up to 100 lbs (45 kg) of fruit, add another ½ cup during fermentation and shorten the maceration time. That is, press well before fermentation completes in order to minimize the extraction of pyrazines.

MY WINE NOW SMELLS OF GERANIUMS

Geraniums are great flowering plants, but alas, a detectable geranium-like smell in wine is considered a serious fault and a winemaking oversight.

What Causes the Problem

The smell of geraniums occurs when potassium sorbate is added to prevent a renewed alcoholic fermentation in wines with residual sugars but which had undergone MLF. Malolactic bacteria still present in the wine cause a series of reactions that gives rise to a substance with the offending smell. It is detectable at very low levels.

How to Assess the Problem

This fault is easily detected as a strong, unpleasant smell of geraniums that masks other aromas.

How to Fix

This fault cannot be reversed or cured, and the wine is best discarded. Don't be tempted to blend it with a perfectly good wine.

How to Prevent

Don't use potassium sorbate in any wine that has undergone MLF.

For wine that will be put through MLF, ferment to total dryness—no sorbate will be required as there will be no residual sugars and the wine will be stable.

For wine that has undergone MLF and which has residual sugars, the only option is higher doses of SO_2 *without* sorbate and to drink the wine young without too much aging before SO_2 drops to low levels.

I UNCORKED A BOTTLE AND THE WINE SMELLS LIKE A WET DOG, THERE ARE NO WINE AROMAS

This problem is called "cork taint" or "corked wine," a condition where wine has lost many of its aromas and flavors and instead has a moldy, musty smell, like that of a damp basement, wet dog, or wet newspaper. This fault almost always, but not exclusively, occurs in wine bottled with natural corks.

What Causes the Problem

Cork taint is the result of microbial contamination of cork material that causes a chemical reaction with chlorine in the environment, or of material that was used in bleaching natural corks in the manufacturing process. It is often referred to as TCA, short for 2,4,6-trichloroanisole, a powerfully odorous substance with an extremely low detection threshold, in the parts per trillion (ppt) range, but it poses no health concerns. It can, however, easily contaminate your winemaking area and infect wine as wood barrels and pallets and cardboard boxes can harbor these contaminants.

How to Assess the Problem

Those not familiar with TCA and corked wine may not recognize this as a fault, if they can even detect it. But, once known, the smell is unmistakable, and it masks all other aromas.

How to Fix

There is no fix for a TCA-infected wine; it is best discarded. There is anecdotal evidence that a few winemakers have had some success in at least reducing the musty smell by pouring wine over plastic wrap made from PVC (polyvinyl chloride)—not LDPE (low-density polyethylene) plastic—although this is believed to scalp other aromas and flavors.

How to Prevent

Given that this fault occurs almost exclusively in wines bottled with natural corks, use a TCA-free alternative closure, such as micro-agglomerates or synthetic closures, if you intend to age wine for years.

Alternatively, consider kegging wine. Wine is protected and "pushed" by inert gas, such as nitrogen or argon; you simply pour as much wine as desired into a carafe for your dinner needs.

Avoid all chlorine-based cleaning or sanitizing products in your winemaking area; these are common, high-risk sources of TCA infections.

I UNCORKED A BOTTLE AND THE WINE SMELLS LIKE A HORSE'S BEHIND

This "problem" is known as Brettanomyces, or "Brett," as it is affectionately referred to, a condition where (almost exclusively red) wine has an unappealing barnyard smell or medicinal, sweaty, "Band-Aid," or rancid aromas. It's not always perceived as a problem, not to winemakers who enjoy the barnyard smell and who find that a little Brett adds complexity. They argue that it is part of their terroir, a grape-growing term that refers to the combination of factors, including soil, climate, and sunlight, which give wine grapes their distinctive character. Others consider any amount of Brett an outright fault.

What Causes the Problem

This fault occurs because of the indigenous *Brettanomyces* yeast that can metabolize tiny amounts of naturally occurring substances into volatile compounds with a range of smells with very low detection thresholds. *Brettanomyces* has strong physiological resistance, so it can persist for very long periods of time, during which it can easily contaminate your winemaking area and equipment.

How to Assess the Problem

The range of smells can vary greatly depending on the *Brettanomyces* strain. They can be generally categorized as animal, savory, woody, putrid, chemical/solvent, veggie, rotting fruit, floral spice, dairy, and earthy—not a good list, which is why most winemakers dread *Brettanomyces* and avoid it at all costs.

How to Fix

Brettanomyces is very difficult to eradicate and can easily propagate across the entire winemaking area. Chitosan (see the section CLARIFYING … AND FINING in Chapter EIGHT) has been shown to be of some help in treating infected wines.

How to Prevent

Assume that *Brettanomyces* yeast is always present and be extra vigilant and practice good cellar hygiene. If you have had a "Brett" infection, consider using chitosan after the completion of MLF as a preventive measure.

Reds are at higher risk because of their greater amounts of Brett-prone polyphenols, higher pH, and because the wines are produced by macerating skins in juice. Ferment to complete dryness—i.e., an SG of 0.995 or lower. Minimize the time to complete the MLF and add sulfite as soon as recommended after the completion of alcoholic and malolactic fermentations. Store and age wine at a cool temperature, ideally at 55°F (13°C).

Index

Where there are multiple page entries, page numbers in **bold** type indicate the most important and relevant references.

NOTES

NOTES